Womenpsalms

Womenpsalms

compiled by
Julia Ahlers,
Rosemary Broughton,
and Carl Koch, FSC

Saint Mary's Press
Christian Brothers Publications
Winona, Minnesota

The poem "Pearls," by Alla Renée Bozarth, appears in *Womanpriest: A Personal Odyssey* (San Diego, CA: LuraMedia, 1988) and in *Stars In Your Bones: Emerging Signposts on Our Spiritual Journeys* (Saint Cloud, MN: The North Star Press, 1990). "Belonging," by Alla Renée Bozarth, appears in *Stars In Your Bones: Emerging Signposts on Our Spiritual Journeys*.

The poem "Two Prayers: Martha and Mary," by Nancy Corson Carter, appears in *Martha, Mary, and Jesus: Weaving Action and Contemplation in Daily Life* (Collegeville, MN: The Liturgical Press, 1992).

The verses from Psalm 139 quoted on pages 5 and 93 are from *Psalms Anew: In Inclusive Language,* compiled by Nancy Schreck and Maureen Leach (Winona, MN: Saint Mary's Press, 1986). Copyright © 1986 by Saint Mary's Press. All rights reserved.

The other scriptural quotations on page 5, and the scriptural quotations on pages 9, 23, 27, and 63 are from the New Revised Standard Version of the Bible. Copyright © 1989 by the Division of Christian Education of the National Council of Churches of Christ in the United States of America. Used with permission.

The scriptural quotation on page 73 is from the Revised Standard Version of the Bible. Copyright © 1946, 1956, 1971 by the Division of Christian Education of the National Council of Churches of Christ in the United States.

The scriptural quotation on page 100 is from the New Jerusalem Bible. Copyright © 1985 by Darton, Longman and Todd, and Doubleday, a division of Bantam, Doubleday, Dell Publishing Group.

The publishing team included Carl Koch, FSC, development editor; Barbara Bartelson, typesetter; Evy Abrahamson, cover artist and illustrator; McCormick Creative, cover designer; pre-press, printing, and binding by the graphics division of Saint Mary's Press.

Printed in the United States of America

Printing: 6 5 4 3 2

Year: 1999 98 97 96 95 94 93

ISBN 0-88489-287-5

Contents

Preface

Some years ago, Saint Mary's Press published a small book entitled *Praying Our Experiences.* In that book, the author urged readers to reflect on the everyday experiences in their life and to use their honest reflections as a way of prayer. *Womenpsalms* calls its readers to much the same realization and challenge, for its poems, prayers, and anecdotes are indeed prayerful reflections on the authors' everyday experiences as Christian women in the 1990s.

These "womenpsalms" cover a wide range of experiences: giving birth, baking bread, playing with children, hiking the Appalachian Trail, and even facing death. The emotions expressed in these womenpsalms span the spectrum as well: solidarity with all women—past, present, and future; anger over the discrimination against women by the church; grief and pain due to the breakup of a marriage; joy and celebration over the discovery of personal strength; and thanksgiving for special persons or moments in life.

Though this collection is not meant to be read in a necessarily linear fashion, we have tried to weave the selections into a pattern that flows from solidarity to anger, grief, and pain; from anger and pain to hope and courage; from hope and courage to celebration and thanksgiving; and from celebration and thanksgiving back to solidarity. The selections are indexed by topic to help you locate pieces for specific occasions. We hope that you find this useful.

Such a wide array of selections makes this volume a versatile resource for personal prayer and reflection, group gatherings, or special prayer services. *Womenpsalms* can be used to foster a sense of solidarity among women across the generations, to send an affirming message to the next generation of women about respecting themselves and trusting their experiences. Though *Womenpsalms* is by women, it is not solely for women. Men who are sensitive to women's experiences or who want to become more sensitive will appreciate the breadth and depth of this collection. The selections can serve as a bridge between the sexes and open up communication on difficult topics. Couples can pray and reflect on the selections together. *Womenpsalms* can also bring the voice of women into your church community through using a selection as an opening prayer or petition during Sunday worship.

Suggestions for Enjoying *Womenpsalms*

Read meditatively. Each selection offers a special insight into the experience of women. Take your time reading. If a particular phrase touches you, stay with it. Relish its feelings, meanings, and concerns.

Give *lectio divina* a try. This type of meditation is "divine studying," a concentrated reflection on the wisdom of the writing. Read the selection once. Then concentrate on one or two sentences, pondering their meaning for you. Then read the piece again, slowly and meditatively. Follow this reading by offering a prayer or carrying on a conversation with God in reaction to the reading. Finally, read the selection once more, and then compose your thoughts about it. *Lectio divina* commonly ends with the formulation of a resolution.

Lectio divina may be done as a group prayer by reading each selection out loud. Special lines, insights, and feelings could be shared after each respective reading.

Undertake some journal writing. Writing is a process of discovery. Each woman who contributed to these womenpsalms gained valuable insights just from the act of writing. If you write for any length of time, stating honestly what is on your mind and in your heart, you will unearth much about who you are, how you stand with your God, what deep longings reside in your soul, and more. If you have never used writing as a means of prayer, try it. After you have spent time with a selection, write your response in some form, like a letter back to the author, a poem, a song, or a dialog with God.

Our Thanks

With deep respect and appreciation, we thank all the women who contributed selections for *Womenpsalms*. Making the final selections was one of the toughest yet most rewarding tasks for us as editors. While reading each selection, we were overcome with a sense of reverence at the realization that we were holding a part of each writer's soul in our hands. We regret we could not publish all the selections submitted to us.

May the God of Life and Blessing fill our hearts and minds as we receive and contemplate the gifts presented to us in this collection.

Julia Ahlers
Rosemary Broughton
Carl Koch, FSC

Part 1

Two are better than one. . . . For
if they fall, one will lift up the
other. . . . A threefold cord is
not quickly broken.

Ecclesiastes 4:9–12, NRSV

Visitation

Each woman listens.
Each speaks:
Ah! the life within you, within me—
    a new revelation:
    God's saving love
            impregnates
        the universe
            in woman . . .
        joy for the anawim!
        Magnificat!

    Again today
    women tell their
stories to each other—
    magnificat!
    Listen sisters,
        listen brothers.
    A new outpouring.
        This time:
    resurrection!

Mary Southard, CSJ

Shall We Let God's Goodness Fall upon Us?

My dear friends,
shall we let God's goodness fall upon us
like sweet rain—
falling in our mouths,
blending with our tears,
washing, always washing us,
readying us for what is new?

My dear friends,
shall we let God's goodness slide
down our bodies like fragrant oil,
protecting always protecting
even as it softens us,
readying us for what is new?

My dear friends,
shall we let God's gifts of
bread and wine
become our bodies,
feeding always feeding,
even as they comfort us,
and ready us for what is
oh-so-very
new?

Mary A. Bowen

Mother God
Spirit-filled Woman
Source of all living things
It was you who breathed life into me.
In your likeness I was formed.
The darkness of your sacred womb
    enwraps me in the silence of the Holy One.
Your creative energy pulsates
    through every fiber of my being.
You birth forth life within me.
Your abundant breasts continue to sustain my very being.
You carry me close to your heart
    and sing your song of love to me.
You hold me close to you and comfort me.
Cradled in your arms, I am at peace.
You bathe me with life-giving waters of your giftedness.
Reflected in your eyes is my dignity as woman.
You nurture me and guide me
    to proclaim my sacredness as woman of God.
You call me forth to image your compassion, love, and joy
    to a broken world.
Together we dance life's passionate song.

Mary Kemen, OSF

She-God

Where is the She-God
the voice in the night
the beckoning to be
the calling, the namesake
of my feminine spirit.

For i have kissed the altar's stone
carried the cross
lain on the sodden earth
beseeched the heavens
cried tears of the soul.

Where do my words find refuge to speak
when i cannot weave a homily
though my life is a homily
when i cannot bear the chalice and vestments
though my being resounds with
passion-filled clarity which yearns
of active expression.

Where is the She-God
but in my dreams and images

Which beckon me

to discover her ways
within the name of Yahweh
beyond the sanctions known to Mary

Within the grain of the cross
the table of the disciples
the earth of the garden

it is then
my voice is given wings
and my spirit is set free.

Jean M. Gunderson

After All, I'm a Woman

I would guess that the majority of men and women in the world do not think I have a legitimate claim to pursue the ministry.

After all, I'm a woman.

However,
>I did receive a call.
>>So what? So do other people.
>>How do you know God meant *ministry* as *minister*?
>>Maybe you misinterpreted the call.

After all, you're a woman.

>This is true.
>>I'm a woman.
>>>And I cannot *prove* my call beyond offering you
>>>myself and my gifts,
>>>To let you judge for yourself
>>>What God has called me to become.

However,
>If God *has* called me,
>*Why* has God called me?

>Perhaps this is not important to you,
>But *it is* of utmost importance to me.

>For you see,
>>if God can have any man God wants,
>>*why* does God need me?

After all, I'm a woman.

>But then, perhaps that's the key:
>my woman-ness.

What can I offer that no man ever could?
>And beyond that . . .
>What is unique about me that even further separates me
>from every other woman?

As a woman
   every month
   I am forced to be in direct dialog with my body
   whether I want to or not.
   I have the opportunity
   —just by virtue of being a woman—
   to examine myself,
   to cleanse myself,
   to know myself.

As a woman,
   I have the gift
   To allow life to begin *in me.*
   To grow a creation as God did in the very beginning.
   I can participate directly in a Genesis happening
   Because if I choose to, I can be a childbearer,
   A giver of promised potential and hope.

As a woman,
   I am caught in a society,
   a culture,
   a world,
   That for the most part
   Views women
         as the weaker sex
         as the emotional sex
         as the worth-*less* sex.

   I can be manipulated,
   stepped on,
   violated,
   abused,
   replaced . . .

Because,
   After all, I'm a woman.

And you say,
   That's right! Everything you've said so far simply happens
   Because of your being a woman.

But think about it this way:
   Jesus took time to *know* who he was becoming,
   Jesus came so that we can
   be *born* from above, and thus have new *life.*
   Jesus was
      manipulated,
      stepped on,
      violated,
      abused,
      annihilated so as to be forgotten and replaced.

And why did this happen to him?
   After all, he's not a woman.
   After all, he's the Son of God.

Imagine.
   My vulnerability
   and Jesus' vulnerability
   intersect
   at the point
   of womanhood.

Why vulnerability?
   Because knowledge of yourself is growth.
   The ability to create new life involves risk.
   And being weak means letting go of control.

My story and Jesus' story
   intersect
   at womanhood.

I can know Jesus
   know *about* Jesus
   understand Jesus
   in a way *no man* ever will.

After all, I'm a woman.

Now,
   if I have validity as a woman before Christ,
Then
   my gifts have validity for ministry,
For
   Christ affirms me:

My daughter, your faith has set you free.

So, for me in particular,

My gift with language
 can include women
 embrace women
 give permission to *be* women.

My gift of healing can
 allow women to finally stand up
 allow women to no longer hemorrhage
 allow women to kneel and anoint Jesus' feet.

My gift of listening can
 release the centuries
 of pent-up stories
 that women have never been sanctioned
 to reveal.

I can do all of this
Because
After all, I'm a woman.

Already,
 I hear the rumblings
 of the Pharisees:

 This is the SABBATH!
 You have broken the LAW!
 That person is UNCLEAN!
 Have you no respect for GOD!

 STONE HER!
 STONE HER!
 STONE HER!

As the first rock flies
 These words
 echo inside my heart
 and blaze truth throughout my person:

My vulnerability
 and Jesus' vulnerability
 intersect
 at the point
 of womanhood.

A second rock follows the first

　　You are a daughter of Abraham.

A third rock

　　Your faith has set you free.

On the fringes of the crowd,
　　the cloaks of the assailants
　　strewn at her feet,
　　stands a young girl.

She is
　　confused,
　　frightened,
　　and angry.

Is it really *worth* it?
　　She thinks.
Worth *risking* your life for?

They could do this to me too.
　　TO ME.

Her heart stills.

　　SILENCE.

　　Of women
　　from all the quiet places in the world.

And the power of the Holy Spirit
　　Came upon her
　　And she heard the call of God

　　To be a minister.

For
After all
She's a woman.

Joyce Anderson-Reed

A Trinitarian Presence

It was a crisp autumn day. Women had been straggling across the field to the big, century-old, yellow house all afternoon. The community of Bethany House, a Catholic Worker emergency shelter for women and children, was slowly gathering for its weekly celebration of the Eucharist. This loosely knit group was made up of women who were all former guests of the shelter. They came now for support; they came to relieve their loneliness. They came with children tucked two to a stroller in strollers meant for one; they came limping; they came babbling, carrying on conversations only they understood. They came as God's special gift to us, and tonight would be no exception.

Because most of these women came from backgrounds where celebrating birthdays was not economically possible, an important part of the women's weekly gatherings had been the celebration of birthdays, both their own and their children's. Balloons, streamers, presents, cake, and ice cream were all part of the evening. This Wednesday we were celebrating four-year-old Biesha's birthday. Several years ago, Biesha, her mother, and her two brothers were guests of the house when their father was first incarcerated. Now, settled in their own apartment, the family continued to rely on the shelter for emotional and physical support.

Short and slight for her age, Biesha danced around the house, eyes shining, as we prepared to celebrate the liturgy. This, she knew, was to be a special evening for her. Her brown skin gleamed with a soft aura against her crisp new turquoise dress. Secretly, she whispered in my ear that she hoped she would get a Barbie doll for her birthday.

As the drama of the liturgy unfolded, so did the poignancy of the people's prayers. Some prayed to find a job. Others prayed that they could make it again—but this time without drugs. There were prayers, too, for friends still in prison. And there was a special prayer for Biesha, that she might grow gracefully in age and wisdom. As we joyfully shared robust hugs with each other during the exchange of peace just before Communion, I found Biesha had attached herself to my leg like a little vine.

I held this beautiful child in my lap while the eucharistic bread was passed from person to person, while each of us held the host until all could receive together. As I sat on the floor with the Eucharist in my right hand and my left arm wrapped around Biesha, I wondered about the Divine Presence in my midst. I thought of Jesus and his birth into poverty; I thought of his short, abruptly ended life. I thought about Biesha and all that her few years had held already, and I wondered, What will she be like at thirty-three? Was I holding the Divine in my right hand or in my left? And what about the Presence I felt and knew at the core of my very being? There was no answer. God was so real. We were three, but we were One; the Trinity in profound Reality.

Hilary Gutman

Gospel

Sister, do you see? The trees are bleeding
    like the time when I was giving birth
    you stayed all night and through the morning
    gracefully your firm gentle hands
    drew life out of my wounded body

Sister, do you remember? The war is over
    with news of peace down in the clover field
    you came running into the wind with open arms
    our eyes met the emptiness of the sky
    and you surprised me with your laughter

Sister, time is gone but we share our children
    "mine are also yours"
    you said and then you chose to leave
    with tears of joy and hope in sadness
    our lonely hearts together in their games

and now that words are almost nothing
Christ, word of freedom, I call you sister.

Cristina Stevens

A Letter to My Sisters

Strong sisters who have walked with me,
and wept and laughed and soared with me,
Can we not yet on this life's plane
reach out, and up and up again
until by reaching, soaring, searching
at last we find the prize of living life
through women's eyes?

And then by Love and Faith and Grace
we'll share with other waiting hearts
the treasures of this Women's Place.

Deborah B. Sims

Memory

O Holy Memory,
Carry us down the ages
   on threads of remembrance.
Connect us with our sisters
   and mothers of all times.
Bring us their childhood innocence
   and their adolescent hope again.
Recreate the longings of our
   mothers and grandmothers
   before their succumbing
   to the weight of patriarchy.
Touch us with the unfulfilled
   capacities of our foremothers
   whose lost energies we now resurrect.
Gather the light threads
   of anguish and hope
   that bind us together
And weave for us a new memory
   in this time and place.

Evelyn Hunt

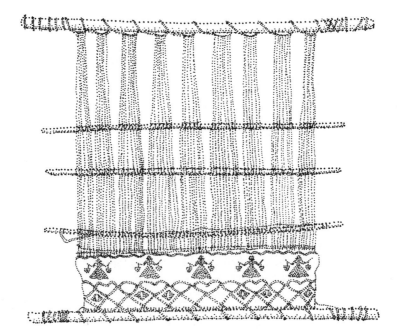

An All Hallows' Eve Homecoming

For over eight years, my prayer group of seven women has gathered weekly to share, discern, and support one another on the Christian journey, and sometimes just to enjoy our solidarity. Upon reflecting about our eight years together, the image came to me of a ritual that symbolized our journey together and our bondedness. I originally wrote this piece as a gift to my prayer group. Now I would like to offer it as a gift to you.

October 31. We walked through the tunnel of oak trees on a path lit by a half-hidden moon. Leaves rustled under our feet as we filed to our gathering. The silver stillness heightened our anticipation. Each of us felt a little off-center, wondering what the night would hold. Comfort came from knowing that we walked with dearly loved friends.

During our years of praying together, the only times we were this silent were when we were listening to or praying for one of the women in our group. In times of painful sharing, we felt free to stop in mid-sentence and breathe deeply to compose ourselves, knowing that in the silence, each of the others embraced us with a warm mantle of prayer, acceptance, and care. Then we could go on with our story.

Usually the first moments of our gatherings were filled with chatting and laughter, a quick social before getting down to planned discussion, reading, and prayerful study. Chairs would be arranged around a table with a candle in the middle—a blessed circle of women coming together to pray, support, and love one another. We were seven different personalities, seven different auras, seven different lifestyles, seven different stories, and seven different gifts to be shared, but through the connecting thread of our growing love of God and each other, we were all entwined by our desire to discover and live fully who we were created to be.

But tonight had indeed started differently! I kept thinking, "Leave it to our hostess to orchestrate something this exotic! A gathering of cloaked women deep in the woods, complete with a hooting owl to mark our passage."

A sharp wind whipped through the woods. We pulled our cloaks more tightly around us. I could not help but wonder at the strange picture we must be making. On this particular night, adults our age usually stayed safe inside homes decorated with paper witches and black cats, ready to hand out sweet treats to neighborhood children clad in costumes.

Our hostess had suggested that as we filed through the woods, we should let the darkness envelop us and remember all women who had been subjected to the dark side of another person, society, or even themselves.

At last we came upon the old converted barn, still looking forlorn on the outside. A lamp illuminated the entrance. As we stepped quickly to the door, an owl swooped past us and into the oak woods.

After silently removing our cloaks, we washed our hands in rose-scented water and dried them on rough towels. Then we reached into a woven basket to withdraw a folded card. After turning off the outside light and locking the door, our hostess also washed and dried her hands and then withdrew the last card. We arranged ourselves around a circular oaken table. The burning apple wood sent incense from the fireplace. A single large candle flickered warmly in the center of the table, where oak leaves were spread to catch any dripping wax.

We had come to remember and celebrate our own seeking and journeying together and the seeking and journeying of all women.

As classical music floated up through the rafters, our hostess asked us to examine our card to see which gift of the Spirit was ours to share this evening with our fellow travelers: wisdom, understanding, counsel, fortitude, knowledge, piety, or reverence. Then we each pinned our card over our heart and, still in silence, joined hands, closing our eyes and bowing our head, while our hostess invited us to journey within to our interior castle, our own sacred center.

We had learned that each of us traveled at her own speed, so we waited for our heart to slow down after that first step. Our meditations together had taught us to trust in our instincts, to let the Spirit move us through our darkness and fear into the bright light within. In our circle, our spirits slowly journeyed inward and began to feel free and light in the letting go. As we reached our own center, we would gently squeeze the hands of the woman on each side. Joined through hands and hearts, the circle of our spirits drew together in the sacred center, pulled by the primeval instinct planted in us at creation.

In the deepening, consoling silence, the sighing trees and trickle of the stream outside seemed to invite us to open our eyes and marvel at our companions. The sighing was our souls in longing, the stream was the living waters within. We had all arrived safe and sound.

Nodding agreement, we stood and then sat in a circle on the floor and lifted our voices, invoking God's love to illuminate our sharing this night, invoking God's light to come into the lives of all people so that the darkness would be banished forever, invoking God's light and love to surround and protect every spirit created from the beginning of time to the end of time, to protect all of creation.

In unison, we raised our voices in prayer:
For women of all ages who have been reviled and labeled as witches or bitches,
for women who have been abandoned,
for women who have been raped or abused in any way—physically, mentally, or emotionally,
for women who have been tortured or murdered,
for women who have been seen as invisible,
for women who have been treated as second-class citizens,
for women devalued for not having a picture-perfect figure,
for women scoffed at for their special gifts of healing and intuition,
for women whose spirits were destroyed or frozen with fright,
for women too busy to find and live their own truths,
for these women and for all people imprisoned by darkness,
we lift our voices and hearts and prayers.
Our hostess opened the Sacred Book and read 1 Corinthians 12:4–11:

Now there are varieties of gifts, but the same Spirit; and there are varieties of services, but the same Lord; and there are varieties of activities, but it is the same God who activates all of them in everyone. To each is given the manifestation of the Spirit for the common good. To one is given through the Spirit the utterance of wisdom, and to another the utterance of knowledge according to the same Spirit, to another faith by the same Spirit, to another the working of miracles, to another prophecy, to another the discernment of spirits, to another various kinds of tongues, to another the interpretation of tongues. All these are activated by one and the same Spirit, who allots to each one individually just as the Spirit chooses. (NRSV)

Then we all thanked and praised this Spirit who gifted us, until silence marked an end to our words. Eyes closed and souls stilled.

In our mind's eye, we walked as to the edge of the pool of living water and gazed at our reflection, being blessed by our own special beauty as a precious child of God, loved and cherished beyond belief. We dipped the blessing cup into the pool and drank deeply, cleansed, refreshed, and ready to let the Spirit speak.

Standing in the middle of our circle, Wisdom spoke; then Understanding, Counsel, Fortitude, Knowledge, and Piety spoke; and lastly, Reverence spoke. Each of us shared the gift of insight, knowing that because of tonight's experience we would never be quite the same. Time held no sway. The blessing cup was filled one last time and passed from one to the other as we recited the closing benediction.

We pledged to gather our circle of spirits again on this most hallowed of eves, to pray and journey together, letting our spirits speak of all that is sacred within us.

With hands joined, we closed our eyes, traveling from our own centers back to the circle of women, back to the barn. We gazed at our sisters with brighter eyes, connected, bonded.

With a wide smile, our hostess stretched her arm up and pulled on a long, black cord. Bushels of bright oak leaves spilled upon each of us and onto the floor. In a fit of celebration we found ourselves tossing handfuls of leaves high into the air or at each other, as the child in each of us laughed and cavorted. Two calico cats, sitting high in the rafters, looked at each other and then stretched their ruffled necks to better see the show below.

And then we reveled, bobbing for apples, playing charades, pulling taffy, and looking for hidden pumpkins. In front of the fireplace, we munched popcorn, sang old songs, and finally settled down to talking about what our life had been about since we were last together, each one of us feeling totally accepted and loved. Oh, what a night!

As the mauve and lavender light of dawn filled the east window, our hostess read her latest poem dedicated to the gathered women who had shared so intimately with her. Then, together, we headed for the kitchen and a huge breakfast of everyone's favorites: toasted home-made bread, raspberry jam, sausage and scrambled eggs, hash browns, muffins, bacon, fresh fruit, juice, coffee, tea. We ate heartily after our traveling, playing, and sharing. The breakfast stretched out as long as we could make it last. We sipped slowly and asked for seconds of coffee or tea, trying to delay our parting.

As the sky grew more and more light, we pitched in to clean up the kitchen, sweeping the leaves outside and making plans to gather together in the near future.

We hugged and blessed each other and, retrieving our cloaks, threw them over our arms as we walked out into the daylight. The leaf-strewn path back seemed but a short walk and our steps far lighter. A new day had dawned, full of sunshine and joy-filled spirits. It was the Feast of All Saints, November 1.

Sharon L. Buettell

Daughters

Daughters of Eve,
When the garden crumbles
Live tenaciously.

Daughters of Sarah,
When times are uncertain
Live faithfully.

Daughters of Pharaoh,
When death is expedient
Live defiantly.

Daughters of Deborah,
When power stumbles
Live prophetically.

Daughters of Ruth,
When love bonds
Live committedly.

Daughters of Esther,
When mores threaten
Live brazenly.

Daughters of Mary,
When the Spirit moves
Live expectantly.

Le Martin

Part 2

My God, my God, why have you
forsaken me?
Why are you so far from helping
me, from the words of my
groaning?

Psalm 22:1, NRSV

Mid-Life

If my goal
is to be whole

I cannot evade
the pain of Your flame.

Before the remolding
comes the meltdown.

Jeanette Blonigen Clancy

To My Children on the East Coast with Their Father

My neighbor said that while we were at Grandma's house
in California for a month,
it was like the neighborhood closed down for a while.
Now that you have left,
my heart has closed down.
I didn't expect it to do that.
I looked forward to the quiet,
to the milk cap staying on the jug,
to the front door remaining closed;
I wanted a night when I could watch
whatever I wanted on TV.
You called and said you were having lots of fun
and that Daddy's new wife was really nice,
and I said good.
When I hung up, I wept for your joy and my losses.

Elizabeth Alexander

The Second Good-bye

I don't remember
  the first good-bye.

At some point
  he walked
  through the door
  divorced.
  (He remembered)
  I only know . . .

He wasn't there.

I missed his coming
  and going.
The ordinary days
  cheerios in the mornings,
  snacks before bed.
The celebrations
  of life and death.
  birth days
  family funerals
  retirement
  Christmas
We never shared
  the promise
  of a new year
  because . . .

I wasn't there.

And he missed me
  although "it wasn't
  right," he said.
  he felt
  loss
For my extraordinary days.
  parties
  sweet sixteen
  dates
  graduation
  my first job

We never shared
  a single step
  along the
  wedding aisle.
How to "give
  away" what . . .

wasn't his?

Our lives did touch
  too seldom.
  fleetingly.
  a movie
  a meal
Visits now and then,
  a game of cards
  a phone call
  and letters.
Missals of fatherly love
  across the miles
  across the years
  (I miss them so)
Those simple epistles
  formed a bond
  that salved
  the absence
  for father and
  the daughter . . .

Who wasn't there.

But love united
  in an infirmary.
Love embraced.
  held hands,
  and grasped
  the healing.
Then wholeness.
  Sad, yet
  joy-filled
  for all eternity.

For love's a gift
  no less
  when given
  in quietus.
  Agape
  conceived
  before that
  second and
  final
  good-bye.
I'll always remember
  our farewell.
  that time of
  light
  and grace.

Perhaps because
  for once,
  at least . . .

We both were there.

Pat Mings

The Day Mama Cried
by the Pinball Machine

When Daddy agreed
To cut a deal on
A pinball machine,
There was question
Whether it was for us,
His children, or for him.
But his access to the
Pinball machine was
Quickly outmaneuvered
By three adolescent
Boys, my brothers,
And their friends.
And in the end,
The question of who,

And what, and why
Faded away as slowly
And unpretentiously as
Would the career of
A soldier named
Douglas MacArthur.

The pinball machine was
Housed in the basement,
Which had surrendered
Its space graciously to
My brothers and friends,
Who never left it and
Were conspicuously absent,
Except for school, meals,
Taking out the garbage,
Smoking cigarette butts
In the cornfield,
And letting other boys
In and out the door.

And whether it seemed
Gradual, or abruptly
Overnight, who can say?
Boys' games stepped
Aside for men's . . . and
The Korean War took
Two boys, my brothers,
And most of their friends,
Leaving one brother,
Who, both eventually and
Simultaneously, entered
Med school and was
Called "draft dodger."

FORWAAAAARD MARCH!
FIIIIIRE!!!

Meanwhile in the
Basement, who could
Say how, or why,
Or when, the pinball
Machine became
Lodged against the
Wall, closest to the
Washing machine, and

Gradually settled in,
Taking on the duty
Of family interchange.

"Patty, could you cut
The beans for supper?
They're in a pan on
The pinball machine."

"Leo, someone stopped with
Radio equipment for you.
I told them to leave it
On the pinball machine."

"I came across some
Magazines you might like.
They are down on the
Pinball machine."

"Judy, I left your
Towel and swimming
Suit on the pinball
Machine!" "Thanks, Cathy."

"I'm getting ready
To wash. If you have
Laundry, leave it on
The pinball machine."

"Mary Ann, have you
Seen my Dolly?"
"You left it on the
Pinball machine, Micki."

And so the days
Turned like wheels
Into months, and
Rare was the day
With no reference to
The pinball machine,
Which surreptitiously
Became a backdrop
For the drama,
Both the tragic and
Comic happenings, in
The lives of the family.

A long while later,
Or was it actually
A shorter time,
Who can say?
But later, and before
Both boys put the
Korean War behind,
And before the other
Boy had "MD" cut
Into his name pin,
One of the "war"
Boys died. . . .

Mama, while dazed,
Functioned automatically,
In the maze of
The details of living.
While never laughing,
She also never cried,
Passing from day to
Day like a shadow,
A body trying to
Entertain a mind
Hit with a double
Load of buckshot.

One night, hearing
Muffled crying coming
From the basement,
I sensed without
Seeing that it was Mama.
Descending the stairs
Quietly, slowly, my
Heart hammering from
Fright, I saw the
Sight of Mama crying.
Absorbed in grief,
Leaning with bent
Elbows, hands cupping
Her cheeks, her tears

Slipping drop by drop,
Dripping like blood
From a broken heart,
Onto the pinball machine.

I grew up a mite
That night, never again
Leaving anything on
The pinball machine.
Who can say why,
Or how, or whether it
Was because Mama's
Tears made it sacred,
Or because it was too
Strong a reminder of
Just what Michael's
Death cost, or whether
It was neither.
For who can ever
Define when the line
Is crossed, making
An object sacred,
And therefore a relic?
Is . . . .
It when? . . . .
A child dies . . . . ?
A Mama cries . . . . ?
Or when an object . . .
Sits by respectfully
Offering its homeyness,
Knowing home will
Never be the same
As when three boys
And their friends
Never left the
Basement, except
For . . . .
And war . . . .

Cashel Weiler, OSF

It Hurts!

"Ouch! Ooow, he's hitting me!"
"The man is hurting the woman," is the explanation
    given in a somber but matter-of-fact way
    by a beautiful little seven-year-old
    as she manipulates the male and female
    dollhouse figures.
"She doesn't have to let him continue hurting her," I offer.
"Oh, yes, she does. See, he is bigger than her," is her determined
    response. And the figures are compared side by side:
    proof of dominance and strength.
I try again, "She could ask for help."
    Her large eyes widen,
    incredulous of my naivete.
"Then he will follow us in a car and run us down," she responds
    with knowledge from past experiences
    etched in her memory.

Those eyes continue to haunt me
    eyes of a child
    reflecting the haunting truth of
    pain and experiences of a lifetime
    a lifetime far beyond her seven short years
    experiences which say,
        "you are not safe"
        "there is no one to protect you"
        "men are allowed to hurt women"
        "the big can harm the small"
        "pretty girls get hurt."
    The rage and frustration well up within like a tidal wave gathering
energy before exploding its vengeance upon the shore. I too want to
explode with rage, to spew my vengeance upon an unfair world.
I want to scream at the man
    the brutal man
    the man who has savagely beaten her mother
    the man who has verbally ravaged every female he sees
    the man who has raped her body and soul.
I also want to scream at the woman
    the woman who is mother
    the woman who herself is victim
    the woman who returns again and again to the violence
        with the child
        to the brutal man
    the woman who does not protect her child.

I want to scream at society
a society that endorses violence
as its right and privilege
a society that loudly proclaims equality for all
while simultaneously plugging ears
and closing eyes to the inequalities
that do not affect the privileged group
a society that doesn't hesitate to condemn
someone who steals a child's bike
yet cannot decide to hold a man responsible
for sexually abusing a nonresisting child.
I want to scream at the courts
the courts who do not believe the testimony of the child
the courts who allow the violence to continue
by protecting the brutal man
by allowing him to continue to see the child
without offering the child protection
by their own refusal to prosecute
the man's violent acts.
I want to enfold, protect, hide the child.
I am enraged by my own impotence
my own helplessness
my own powerlessness
to protect the child.

Weeping Mother of all the wounded children, grant me the wisdom
and control to use my rage to help the children. Transform my rage
into the power of love with its ability to creatively bring about change.
May that energy enable me to gather the institutional forces of society
together—including the courts, law enforcement officials, churches,
schools, and families—to enfold the children with the love, care, and
protection that every child is entitled to by birth. And beyond all that,
may I draw strength from the gentle, loving, healing power whirling
within all of your creation, a mighty power that transcends the power
of the veil and the distorted intentions of humankind.

Anita R. Coverdale-Paulson

Husk

To find God
You go into the
Desert and wait.
You won't need to divest yourself—
The desert will do that for you.

Those who live there know that
God loves the dead
The skeletons, the
Dried-up things bleached and scoured
Down to color of earth
Color of sand.

God wants to hold you up and
Listen to the sound the wind makes
Blowing through you,
Will teach that sound to you as your own
The only thing that makes you different.

But first God wants your bones,
Your thirst and hallucination.
By choosing this road you have
Made yourself available,
And the lesson involves economy.

Andrea Cook Cockrell

Lament

Beloved, come.

How long until you come?

I see you, woman, on the cross.
I look for your wounded side,
but see instead a gaping gash, ragged,
where your womb should be.

Wounded womb,
Earth womb,
ragged, as if an explosion has torn you apart;
a war has raged in you
and ravaged you.
Gone
   your fertility,
waning
   your creativity,
flowing
   your life's blood.

And I?
I snarl and hiss
and fight the shackles they would put on me.
I kick and scratch authority
whose words to me always sound like "ought" and "should."

I battle with the very air
but no one ever really responds.
Authority looks the other way
or pays me pious, fraudulent lip service.

Wearied by the words,
spent by the conflict,
I turn in to my heart
and find once more your woundedness,
which is the same as mine.

Beloved, come.
How long until you come?
Come.
I long to enfold you in my arms.

Antoinette Roeder

Absalom

I was fourteen   just barely
good student   painfully shy
conscientious   attended every
required sex education class
got pregnant on my first date
(he treated me oh-so-tenderly)

He wasn't one whit tender when
I screamed for endless hours and
almost died before giving birth
to our baby   He slipped out of
town so *he* wouldn't miss his
first exciting week of college

My higher education consisted of
sore nipples diaper rash and colic
An elective in bottles and needles
came later   too late   they called
told me he's dead at Fourteenth and
K Street   my child of fourteen   my son

Robin Stratton, OCD

Short-Term Memory Loss

What am I doing in the grocery store parking lot?
I was on my way to church.
This is not your simple standing in front of the refrigerator—
door wide open, mind blank!
We're talking serious lapse of memory.

Well, God, have I ever told you how grateful I am
that this grocery store is so nearby?
That each time I visit here I feel nourished,
poor (but not in Spirit), refreshed, excited about
creating something special for my family?
We do have some things in common . . . like you said.

I'm so glad that I happened upon this parking lot.
I may never have taken the time to tell you that
apples are a fantastic creation. And bread!

The bakery here is getting very specialized.
I think I'll take advantage of their special on grapes, today.
Talk to you later . . . God!

Annamarie Burtness

Quotidian

An average American teenager,
I am terrified!
I don't know where I am.
Bright sunlight
Is streaming through the window;
But I don't know what time it is,
Or what day it is.
He is there with me,
But I can't see his face.
He tells me everything is all right
And I am a good girl.
But I have pain,
So much pain!
Horrifying tears
Stream down my cheeks.
Each time I move
The pain in my back
Pierces like a sword.
My head is throbbing
Like a board has crossed my skull.
Again he tells me I am okay.
And we will wash away the evidence
So no one will ever know.
Finally I find the telephone
But the line is dead.
I stumble toward the door
But he blocks my way.
My body is fiercely jerking
In uncontrollable spasms.
And now,
Thirty years later,
The nightmares begin again.

Karen F. Duh

Sarah and Hagar

Sarah: I am called Sarah. My name means "princess."
Hagar: I am called Hagar. My name means "flight."

Sarah: I am Hebrew.
Hagar: I am Egyptian.

Sarah: I am Abraham's wife.
Hagar: I am Sarah's slave.

Sarah: I was barren; I had no value as a woman.
Hagar: I was fruitful; I had no value as a woman.

Sarah: But God promised that I would be fruitful. I laughed.
Hagar: I received no promise. I cried.

Sarah: But I could not bear my husband a child. So I chose to give my slave to my husband to be his concubine. Perhaps I would have sons through her.
Hagar: I was not given a choice. I was forced to bear my master a child.

Sarah: When my slave became pregnant, she grew prideful. She looked upon me with disdain.
Hagar: I have no pride.

Sarah: I was outraged.
Hagar: I was despised.

Sarah: My husband told me that my slave was in my power. I could do as I wished with her.
Hagar: I had no power. I could not do as I wished.

Sarah: I beat her.
Hagar: I fled.

Sarah: She came back in submission.
Hagar: God sent me back to submit to my mistress's abuse.

Sarah: Hagar bore a son. He was the son of a slave woman.
Hagar: I bore a son. My master named him Ishmael, meaning "my God hears me." Does my God hear me?

Sarah: My God heard me, and I bore a son. My husband named him Isaac, meaning "laughter." All who heard of my joy laughed with me.

Hagar: I cannot laugh. I have no joy.

Sarah: I saw the slave child playing with my son. I told my husband to drive them out. No slave will share my son's inheritance.

Hagar: We were driven into the desert with only a loaf of bread and a skin of water. When the water was gone, I sat and waited for my child to die.

Sarah: No slave will share my son's inheritance.

Hagar: But God heard our cry and took pity on us. "Arise," God said, "and take the boy by the hand; for I will make of him a great nation."

Sarah: No slave will share my son's inheritance.

Hagar: When I opened my eyes, I saw a well of water. We drank and returned to Egypt. God was with my son as he grew. He became the father of a great nation.

Sarah: God was with my son as he grew. He became the father of a great nation.

Hagar: I conceived my son in slavery. Now, I am free.

Sarah: I conceived my son in freedom. Why don't I feel free?

Hagar: [*Turning to Sarah*] We are mothers of great nations. We are equal.

Sarah: [*Turning to Hagar*] We are mothers of different nations. How can we be equal?

Hagar: If we become sisters, and no longer despise one another, then we shall bring forth great nations. We will all be equal. [*Holds out her hand*]

Sarah: We will not be sisters until we are equal. [*Takes her hand*]

Sarah and Hagar: [*Holding hands and turning to front*] We will not be equal until we are sisters.

Kay Murdy

Leah's Tent

Who has not heard of Laban's trickery
and Jacob's shame in being foisted
a squinting girl. . . .
A curse, to be the elder daughter
without beauty.

My mother—
when the wedding garments
were prepared for me—
sat holding Rachel's hand,
my father saying hurry,
hurry, and adding one more veil;
he warned me not to speak till morning.

Always the wailing
is for Jacob's seven years of cheated hire
among my father's flock.
Who cries for me, silent
on my bridal bed, dreading daylight
as he moved above me

moaning, Rachel, Rachel
ah, Rachel.

Elizabeth Mische John

Uma

You left her on a street in Seoul,
At four months, I was told.
You must have tried to nourish her.
You had your body—nothing more.

It was months before I claimed her.
The airport was our labor room.
My heart pounded when I saw her,
And my mother-spirit rose.

But in my home she cried for you,
Though I had apricots and plums.
"Uma, Uma," she sobbed nightly,
And never settled in my arms.

At seventeen her opposition
Tears the most resilient heart.
"She cannot bond," the experts tell me,
"So let her go—it's not your fault."

"It's not my fault," I tell my friends,
And rage at unrequited love.
She drifts in dark and scary spaces,
And locks each door she passes through.

And so I shed my expectations,
Work at detachment every day.
There are techniques that one can follow,
Groups of others who know the way.

But in the night I am awakened;
An image pierces through my dream.
There is a mirror, we are reflected
Mother, daughter—we look the same.

Her face, serene, shows no difference,
But slowly, slowly, I see my own.
My eyes are changed, my skin is tawny,
I am Korean. Her smile knows.

Oh, Uma, Uma, can you hear us?
Are you there to share our pain?
Our separate needs encircle you,
We call your mother-spirit in.

Nancy Fitzgerald

Comadres *in the Plaza*

Religion is bloodless in the north, neat
and clean, like a white plaster
Pietà, but in this Guatemalan highland
plaza, where the *comadres* stand like carved
stelae with mementoes of the disappeared,
our Lenten devotions come to life.

We explore the places where death entered
in, where the brown hands of the mothers
linger—the protruding bones, the crushed
skulls, the bloody holes where life
leaked out. We tug and pull
the blanket around the corpse shifting
crazily on the path to a shallow grave.

The ancient Maya lived in the mouth
of the jaguar, but these Indian women
ride its back, letting the *ladinos*
of the world worry about the steam
rising from encircling volcanoes, more
than enough to rock the ground of the proud
and to redeem the dream of the innocent.

Jane McDonnell, BVM

While I Wept

The day had been a long one for me,
And for the first time in my life
I felt completely helpless and alone.
Sitting on the edge on an examining table,
Enshrouded in a paper-napkin gown
I sat terrified and weary from a constant surge of tears.
Fiercely, intensely, yet ever-so-subtly,
Manifestations of malignant growth
Were growing inside of me.
I sensed with reality the present threat of death.
Why had God permitted this dreadful catastrophe?
My memory tried to reconstruct the whole scenario

From the moment my oncologist
Had announced his first suspicions
Until this present diagnosis.
His sincere compassion seemed a feeble attempt
And had not minimized the forceful blow.
When he gently held my face between soft and caring hands,
I knew he sensed my irremediable grief,
The crushing of life's hopes and plans.
It was then I found myself experiencing a peculiar vision.
The words he spoke, enlarged in letters upon a banner,
Seemed to stretch across the sky.
LYMPHATIC CANCER—MALIGNANT!
I was positive I would die.
He left me alone while I wept.
The day was drawing to a close,
And in the lingering silence of the night,
My agony became heaviness weighing on my soul.
This present trial of my faith
Exemplified how weak it really was.
Still overcome by deep despair,
Unable to revive my hope,
I felt powerless. My strength was gone.
And thus dismayed, I prayed.
In those next transforming moments,
By some miracle of grace
I believed God had destroyed the power of death's sting.
And though still weak and faltering,
I knew God would understand
If I tried to trust the divine purpose and go the way God planned.
My little faith, a mustard seed—
Was big enough to see me through.
In the peaceful stillness I was strangely drawn to God,
Who filled me with new courage when mine was all but gone.
God showed me a path to greater faith,
A winding, lonely, tear-filled path,
And I stood amazed when I realized
It was the path that I was on!
God stayed with me while I wept.

Georgina M. Freed

Can This Really Be Me?

I'm forty-four years old.
Breast cancer, how can that be?
Am I numb? No, not really.
I've had a long time
to ponder this dreaded disease.
Mom's first biopsy came
when I was a child of thirteen.
I feared for her life;
I feared for my own.
I was grown,
Pregnant with my first child,
living far away from home,
when that dreaded fear became
Mom's forced reality.
She was in her late fifties.
I'm barely mid-forties.
It's not fair.
I've had no warning.
Suddenly life is a white sterile maze.
Internists, oncologists, surgeons,
anesthesiologists, radiologists—specialists.
It's all so fast, no time to think.
It's tense, dull, listless hours of waiting.
Why me, O God, why me?
Not now, I've far too much to do.
I'm young.
My children are not grown.

The mutilating surgery is done.
My symmetry is gone.
I feel so very lopsided, so unfeminine.
What once was soft and round,
filled with delicious, sensuous feelings,
is now bony, taut, and flat,
devoid of all earthy pleasure.
Will Ed still love me?
Will he still find me attractive?
O God, help us survive as a couple.
Help me in accepting my new body.
It's so strange, like some alien creature.
Is this really me?
My beautiful red hair is leaving me,

handful by daily handful.
Drugs, endless drugs.
Can they possibly find another vein?
My monthly flow is aborted—
forced chemical menopause.
Nausea is overcoming me.
Still I gain weight and grow weak.
Who dwells within this breathing corpse?
It can't really be me!

I've graduated now; I'm a survivor.
It's been one of the harder lessons
in the school of life.
What did I learn?
Well, redheaded wigs are hard to find
and a blonde I'll never be.
But a son of fourteen
making his first tackle in the kitchen
preparing the family's evening meal,
is truly a wonder and a delight.
The interior struggles were far more difficult.
I'm a woman in ministry,
I've been trained to be the giver.
A gracious receiver was not to be my role.
Anger, self-pity, despair enveloped my diagnosis.
As these feelings subsided,
peace had to be made with my God.
Communication with Ed was strained, too.
We tried hard to protect each other,
afraid of the future;
afraid it might hurt too much.
We each stood before the inevitability of death;
the awareness of our mortality was inescapable.
Gradually acceptance arrived;
that's not to say I am ready to embrace death,
No, not yet.
For now I want to swallow life whole,
dance and sing, climb the highest mountain,
savor silence with my God,
break away from the social chains
that once held me captive.
Yes, it's hard to believe
But it is really me.

Hilary Gutman

Good Friday

My landlady, eighty-nine, struggles not to cry
as I leave her. Without the tenant conscience upstairs
to hear, the nurse's aide sent by the state
will scream, and she will be afraid.
I feel this vacation is a betrayal.

This road heads east.
It is one arm of the Cross
that points in all directions,
extending for centuries. The guardrail
forms an endless succession of crosses,
and, beyond it, each reflector is a Station.

I am going home for Easter.
My mother and I will admit
all that we have hidden
over long distance. I will visit
my cousin with the premature baby born this week,
and my ninety-three-year-old friend who broke her hip
a month ago. She will tell me of the hospital,
of the drug addict in the next bed
who screamed.

Winter follows my path although it's April;
hail stings the car;
snowflakes shatter into spittle.
Wetness blurs the front of the windshield
and the back of my eyeglasses. I follow
the lines in the darkness, briefly
cleared by my headlights. In the loneliness
of the sleet, I pray for a tollbooth,
someone at least to thank me for my money,
maybe smile. There are three hours
to go, and I won't be home till midnight.

April Selley

~

We took Communion to the nursing home,
my friend and I.

Bodies old, tired, worn out, broken, crippled.
Spirits old, tired, worn out, broken, crippled.
Some spirits very much alive.

We enter a room; he is in bed.
The once-virile body is faded, wasted,
seemingly asleep.
"Shall we pass him by?" we wonder.
But we ask, "Would you like to receive Communion?"
The eyes open. "Yes," he whispers.
"The Body of Christ."
"Amen." He opens his mouth, receives the host,
has trouble swallowing.
There is a cup of water by the bed.
I put the straw to his lips.
He isn't strong enough to suck.
I hold the cup to his lips and dribble some water
into his mouth. He swallows.
The faded eyes close, open again.
"Thank you," he whispers.

She is in a wheelchair in the hall.
"Would you like to receive Communion?"
"I don't know," she says wistfully.
"I haven't been to Confession lately. I'd like to,
but do you think I should?"
My friend assures her it will be all right,
and she receives gratefully.

She is in a wheelchair, alive, loud.
"Would you like to receive Communion?"
"Come here, let me kiss you." She kisses me.
"And let me kiss you." She kisses my friend.
"Would you like to receive Communion?"
"Yes!" she says loudly. "Amen."
"Come here, let me kiss you."
Her voice follows us down the hall.

We pass several rooms where the residents
are too frail and too weak to respond.
She lies in bed, staring at the ceiling.
"Would you like to receive Communion?"
Her eyes light up.
"Oh, yes," she breathes eagerly, "oh, yes."
"The Body of Christ."
"Amen," she responds, as her aging, wrinkled hand
makes a reverent, slow, deliberate
sign of the cross.
"Oh, thank you, thank you."

We have taken Communion to the residents
of the nursing home,
my friend and I,
and they have shown us illness, senility, sorrow,
suffering, tears, and weakness.

We have taken Communion to the residents
of the nursing home,
my friend and I,
and they have shown us acceptance, courage,
gratitude, reverence, faith, hope, and love.

We have taken Communion to the residents
of the nursing home,
my friend and I,
and they have shown us
the Body of Christ.

Ruth Kulas

Alzheimer Shadow

The shadow of a man sits at my table,
The shadow of a man shares half my bed.
This thing that came has gutted good and left me
The shadow of a man who isn't dead.

I know that shadows make the brightness brighter—
Define the edge of every shaft of light.
Without the velvet darkness at the day's end,
The stars could not appear so bright and white.

Now when he smiles it's like a shaft of lightning.
I love a spark of how he used to talk.
But, oh, this thing is daily stealing, stealing,
Like drops of water wear away a rock.

And as I walk my deeply shaded valleys,
The evil thing I fear is always nigh.
But thou art with me shining in the shadows,
My comfort is thy light that will not die.

Jean M. Wood

Beloved Woman/Child

Child/Woman within the bed
Never at ease in the body and mind of an adult
Always wishing to remain a child
    cared for
    made comfortable
    secure
    responsibility of others
Now death draws near
The body bears no signs of youth
    wrinkled
    frail
    twisted
    wasted
Yet the eyes are still those of a helpless child
There is a longing for something
Something far beyond what I can provide
Mother/Child within the bed
Perhaps the time is close
    for you to rest in the loving arms
    of your Mother/Father God
Perhaps the time of innocence and peace draws near
    to enfold you in its warmth
I will know the time, for a sparkle will return to those
    vacant
    pleading
    hollow eyes
Your skin will glow in a youthful softness
    the illusion of smoothness once again

and your face will emanate the
   peace and beauty of a sleeping child
      free of pain
      free of care
      free of worry
released to the reality of a world beyond our experience
Go, beloved child of age
That is where you belong
I will miss you
   but
I will rejoice in your release
   and in the beauty of your journey
I do not wish to hold you to me
Rather, I surrender you
to the loving care of our Gentle Creator
   to be born anew

Anita R. Coverdale-Paulson

Living Without Mom

My mother died last year. Even as I write this sentence, I find it difficult to believe that she really died. It still feels dreamlike—unreal—unfocused.

I never knew any one event could so change my life like losing my mother. Maybe it was because I was pregnant. Being forty years old and six months pregnant, I simply was not prepared to lose my mother. I needed to talk about feelings of hope for this baby and feelings of fear about motherhood after age forty.

And yet, are any of us ever ready to lose our mothers? Having a mom meant I could still be my mother's little girl at times. I could still call simply to say I was sick, and I knew she would comfort me with words, even though she couldn't comfort me with her presence.

Having a mom meant having a number-one cheerleader. Mom was the first to notice new articles I had written. Even before I knew something had been printed, she would call saying she had seen and read my article and thought it was terrific. I knew hers was a biased reading, but don't we all need someone who thinks what we do is the best that can be done? Moms do that—at least, my mom did!

What has life been like without my mother? Even with the assurances of faith, there is a hole in my heart that will never be filled in the same way that it was filled with the presence of my mom. I live with the assurance that her life was a blessing in birth, in death, and in resurrection, but all things considered, sometimes that isn't enough.

I've spent a year being angry. Mom's life ended when she should have had at least twenty more years to enjoy her marriage, her children, and her grandchildren. I know that however good his life may be, Bradford has missed out on knowing a grandma who unconditionally loved her grandchildren and felt "grandma" was the sweetest name in all the earth.

I still want to shake my fist at God and cry out, "It isn't fair." But I also breathe many prayers of thanks for being gifted with a mother who was kind and caring and lived her faith in words and in deed. I know how rare it is to have a mother who allowed me to live my own life without trying to live her dreams through me. I know how wonderful it is to have a mother who understood children and played with her children and her grandchildren, enjoying each lived moment. I know how lucky it is to have a mother who, through her own deep love for God, led all of us near to God.

My mother. My example. My mentor. My friend. I can do nothing else than claim the blessings you gave to me. I can do no more than hope that my children will claim the same blessings from me.

MaryJane Pierce Norton

Liturgy

All the way to Elizabeth
and in the months afterward,
she wove him, pondering,
"This is my body, my blood!"

Beneath the watching eyes
of donkey, ox, and sheep
she rocked him, crooning,
"This is my body, my blood!"

In the moonless desert flight
and the Egypt-days of his growing
she nourished him, singing,
"This is my body, my blood!"

In the search for her young lost boy
and the foreboding day of his leaving
she let him go, knowing,
"This is my body, my blood!"

Under the blood-smeared cross
she rocked his mangled bones,
re-membering him, moaning,
"This is my body, my blood!"

When darkness, stones, and tomb
bloomed to Easter morning,
she ran to him, shouting,
"This is my body, my blood!"

And no one thought to tell her:
"Woman, it is not fitting
for you to say those words.
You don't resemble him."

Irene Zimmerman, SSSF

Sibling Rivalry

O Mother Church,
I found out today—
You are not our mother at all.
I suspected it all along:
My sisters and I are your
Cinderella stepdaughters
Adopted at birth.

You say you love your
Children equally, but
I know better because
The boys get all the toys:
Colorful vestments
Scented oils
Fire
Water
Wine
Bread
Incense
Golden vessels
Big red books
Magic words
Special powers.

O Mother Church,
If you love us every one,
Why are the girls' most

Important jobs
Setting the altar
Clearing the altar
Cleaning the vessels
And washing the linens?

Well, perhaps I'm
Overstating things.
Sometimes we can
Light the boys' candles
Carry the boys' wine
Read from the boys' books
Pray the boys' prayers
Teach people what the boys think
And distribute to people
What the boys make—
But only sometimes,
In some places,
When the boys say it's okay,
Which isn't very often.

Sometimes some boys
Hate us
And we know why.
They hate us because
They cannot touch us and
Retain their power.
Ah.

They hate us for
Our round hips and
Our soft breasts
And our wet velvet insides,
But most of all they hate us
Because we can do without
Their special toys
And they know it:
We do our
body magic
in the dark
by moonlight
with blood
they will
never taste.

Mary A. Bowen

My Belief

I used to believe that the church was the
    bridge between God and my spirituality.

What I found was that the church was an enemy
    against those whose language it did not represent:
    the wrong sex, the wrong color, the wrong status.

In church, I showed my face to God.
And He did not accept me because I
    was beaten, bloody, and angry.

I cried and I yelled, "How can you abandon me?
    You stuck-up old white man!"
And I was violated more because of my past,
    and where my feet had trod.

I begged the church to love me but they refused
    to sing to all humanity.
I asked the church for forgiveness but they kept reading
    scriptures that told me I was unclean.
I told the church I had been violated and
    the minister had me kneel.
I sung unto the church a song but
    my voice was not heard.
I worshipped among the people but
    no one acknowledged me.
I cried among the church, "Hear my cries!"
    But no one heard.

And I ran out the doors, and I ran, and I ran,
    till I saw a vision of a woman,
    beaten, abused, her clothes torn.
There were scars on her face, bruises on her body,
    tears in her eyes. "Come to me," she said, "I will give you rest."

And I looked in her eyes and asked, "Who are you?
    Why should I trust you?"
And she said, "Because I am among the abused also.
I am among the abandoned, the homeless, the violated.
The wounds on my body mark each time a
    woman is raped, each time a child is abused, each time
    a person is violated.

"I know your pain. For I have been there too.
    Oh, my child, I know your hurt and your suffering.
    I am so sorry.
    Look in my eyes and let me love you.
    Know that you, too, are a child of mine.

"And I also know your heart, your dreams, your desires.
    I know your frustrations,
    I know what you want to become. . . .
    A person of peace, of beauty, of worth."

And we cried together. And embraced each other.
We cleansed each other's wounds, and with tears in our eyes,
She listened to me.
She heard my songs, She sung along.
And we worshipped together, and my body grew tall,
    and my soul ignited with fire.

There was chaos, and She became a blur.
And then She became a flame and entered my life.
And I realized the woman before me was
    my Creator, the source of my existence.

"Go in peace," my heart spoke.
    For She said, "I am with you always."
"Go in love," my soul spoke.
    For She said, "You were conceived with promises."
"Go in self-dignity," my being spoke.
    For She said, "You were mirrored of my image.
    Rise and trust yourself."

I believe that the Creator of my life is
    the bridge between me and my spirituality;
    And that She has become the foundation of my life.

Beth A. Cooper

~

While we've been here begging,
　　we've watched as the men who hold it all
　　close in protective enclaves
　　in fear of the scavengers and looters
　　we're likely to become.

While we've gone around begging,
　　we've been shamed by the flaunting
　　of those who have it all:
　　lush ceremonies of monsignorship
　　and the dubbing of deacons to duplicate
　　males: mimics and shadow of gesture and words.

While we've sat here begging,
　　we've glimpsed the ugly underbelly
　　of what we believed, in our eager youth,
　　to be so gallant and magnificent.
　　Rotting now for sure
　　in sated isolation.

While we've waited here begging,
　　we've searched the soul of our idleness
　　and seen the seeds of radicalism
　　sprout and spread:
　　ready, on your mark, get set . . .

While we've survived here begging,
　　we've learned a simple lesson:
　　No one was born to be a beggar;
　　brothers and sisters all are we.

And when our begging is done,
　　it must cease for our companions of spirit:
　　the powerless, the stranger, the contagious, and the labeled.
　　No more a sister or brother forced to beg.

While you see us here begging,
　　don't drop your coins of condescension and pass by.
　　If you pause at all, look into our eyes,
　　and understand
　　Everything must change.

While we've been here begging . . .

Clare Nolan

Brother, Will You Listen?

I ask you . . .
Will you listen?
Already
my brother
in your amusement
you think
I prattle
in foolishness
born
of half-baked
Feminist Ideas.

I ask you . . .
Will you listen?
Already
my brother
in your kindness
you smile and
attempt
to "set me straight"
or worse, you
are tolerant.

I ask you,
"Will you listen?"
Already my brother
you turn away
in answer.

Denise M. Colgan, RSM

~

The garden has not been planted
and the rain is coming down

A woods trek in the land of hermitage and sacred beech
yields a fistful of phlox and wild onions

The mayflower twinkles in its frame of dead leaves
She meditated perfectly on a violet
Her words were fragile purple gems

In the garden
asparagus, parsley, and traces of cilantro
tell that I have waited here in a more productive time
I almost remember the place
and I am all dug up

In the kitchen
the woman is scalding milk to bake bread

On the deck
the cat meditates fruitfully

In the barnyard
the haystack is nearly eaten away

My garden has not been planted
and the rain is coming down

Sue B. Ralph

Part 3

Suffering produces endurance,
and endurance produces character,
and character produces hope,
and hope does not disappoint us,
because God's love has been
poured into our hearts.

Romans 5:3–5, NRSV

July Dawn

This murk could hardly be called dawn. After six weeks of humidity and high heat, the sun rose behind a pink-gray cloud bank. From the window in Michael's hospital room, the city is shrouded in the muddy haze of summer pollution. Saint Martin's steeple is there. The men incarcerated in minimum security across the street are leaving to catch rides to go out to work. And two nurses stride down the sidewalk; they talk intently, oblivious to the humidity.

Michael has developed a serious case of mononucleosis. We have been here two days, but his throat is so swollen he won't swallow pain medication. It is my first time at this, and I'm sleep-deprived and weary. Grieving too, at the fact that eight years old is horribly young to learn that there is some suffering you must do alone.

Steve has to go out of town on business. One more time when what I really need is a wife. So I'll find relief in tears early in the morning and then put on the whole armor of Deborah and go start the day.

It is no dawn worth painting. But it is light out there.

Mary Zimmer

Shadow and Sunlight

Only in sunlight
Is a shadow cast,
Yet high noon melts
Outlines. Values blend,
Work slows and stops.
Under wide-brimmed hats,
Vagrants slumber in the sun.

When shadows lengthen,
Evening has begun.
Painters require shadows.
Sorrows also have their use.
Our efforts find new meaning
And a worthy end.

Anita Wheatcroft

Belonging

The small plot of ground
on which you were born
cannot be expected

to stay forever
the same.
Earth changes,
and home
becomes different
places.

You took flesh
from clay,
but the clay
did not come
from just one
place.

To feel alive,
important, and safe,
know your own waters
and hills, but know
more.

You have stars
in your bones
and oceans
in blood.

You have opposing
terrain in each eye.
You belong to the land
and sky of your first cry,
you belong to infinity.

Alla Renée Bozarth

Going Home

Visiting your childhood home must be one of life's most bittersweet paradoxes—anticipation of a place that has stood still in your memory, realization that it has changed and that you have changed, and hope for healing of memories. I am returning from a monumental trip during which I slept in my childhood home for the last time and went through all of my parents' possessions to choose which material memories I wanted to keep. I walked the streets I took to school, had one last visit by the river running by my home, rode a bicycle down back streets, and sat one last time in the choir stall in the Methodist church where I was nurtured. I talked to an old girlfriend as if it had only been an hour since we last spoke. I saw old boyfriends whom I knew I would "die" without as a teenager. Now I feel only Grace saved me from those relationships. They probably feel the same way!

Sometimes the nostalgia was too much, and I had to break away. Indeed, I did come home early, partly because the experience was too intense. I talked to saints, everyday people who are angels unaware—most of whom I saw with new eyes on this last visit. I saw ordinary people who knew secrets I still haven't learned: a ninety-one-year-old neighbor who has battled a fractured hip and breast cancer and who still walks every day to the drugstore at nine each morning to have a cup of coffee with a friend who formerly lived next door. Another neighbor who cares for a ninety-three-year-old neighbor in a nursing home whose only relative is her sixty-year-old son, who is now a street person in New York. A next-door neighbor with a heart of gold who cried when our family left. A widower and recovering alcoholic whose life has been transformed by caring for animals and small children. A high-school friend's mother whose health is failing and who spends most of the year with her out-of-state daughter but returns to her home at least a few weeks each year to "feel her roots." A woman physician who gave her marriage and family a high priority and is now one of the most nurturing physicians I know in an age when it has become more acceptable for women to be objective, focused, and masculine. For me, this last woman is a role model of a woman succeeding in her work, using feminine values of relationship. I am still amazed by the serendipity of our chance meeting at the post office on this last visit. I am constantly amazed by the way God works—throwing people in our path when we need them, if we will only see them or take time to talk to them.

I saw others who are models for a life I fear. I know easily how they got there—the pain was too great to bear. Oh, God, let me see you when I am on that path. Let your light shine in our darkness. Heal our wounds with your tears. Heal us: the alcoholic who only leaves her home to go to the beauty parlor once a week; the businesswoman who awakens at five each morning so she "won't have to dream and deal with her dreams"; the couple whose only relationship in their marriage is convenience.

The miracle of life is the ordinary—the ordinary people in my small hometown who know what everyone else's business is, but who also know what caring is all about. The tragedy of life is also the ordinary—the ordinary people who have retreated or escaped from life's everydayness because of the pain. Life is painful, sometimes unbearable. What turns us into survivors and lovers? I haven't found the answer, but I've met people on this visit who have. God, help me to be one, too.

Joanna Seibert

Word-Filled Days

Out of name-filled days,
Traffic jams,
And neon signs at night,
I search for silence.

Find it—in moments
Stolen out of time
In quiet seclusion
Of a moving car
An emptied classroom,
Waiting for the bells.
Anonymity
Of subway train!
Or doctor's waiting room.

Lonely in crowds,
Companioned by my problems,
I need withdrawal
To briefly, reflectively
Pray myself back
Into the place
Where I belong;
Guided, rejoicing
To celebrate the day.

Anita Wheatcroft

Adventus

Virgin Earth beholds the seed time
   hopeful waiting
   in the dark.

Silent stillness, sometime sadness
   promised coming
   in the dark.

Goddess Earth with lambs and lions
   peaceful watching
   in the dark.

Gentle strength, sometime wonder
   quiet budding
   in the dark.

Woman Earth with heart rejoicing
   mystery growing
   in the dark.

Pregnant heartbeat,
   sometime dancing
   expectation in the dark.

All is still now
   hushed and hallowed
     stirring warmth
   within the dark.

Earth cradles love beyond all telling
   glory, glory
   angels singing
     music ringing
   in the dark.

The past now Present
Comes—the Child
This Wonder Counselor
Prince of Peace
Born of Earth to Dwell
Among Us
   is
   Light Eternal
   in the dark.

Nancy Delia Cushing

Advent

I shiver as I kneel in the damp brown leaves.
Working my trowel, I pry up the cool moist dirt
    and crumble the clods with my fingers.
I reach into the bright mesh bags beside me for the dry
    onion-like nuggets
that purport to be tulips and hyacinths.

Impossible, I say.
And yet . . .

I remember glorious expanses of blood-red tulips,
Lacy beds of sweet fragrant hyacinths.
I marvel that such promise is held in these small brown bulbs,
    and I quicken my work.

Sort by size,
check for mildew,
discard the damaged.
Pointed end up,
bury the best.

Not much sunlight left.
Dry branches scrape against each other
    as the wind picks up.

I smooth the fresh-worked soil
and press my open hands
    against the spongy mass of earth.

Through bleak winter days,
through gray-brown bitterness,
I will watch . . .
and I will work . . .
and I will wait to be dazzled by spring.

Judy Thais

Reflections on Bread

Bread—the word brings many images to mind:
   white bread, rye with caraway, whole wheat,
   biscuits, muffins, sweet rolls, bagels,
   long French loaves, plump raisin loaves,
   white or dark, large or small,
   freshly baked or day-old,
   so different, and yet, all bread.

How can I bring bread,
how can I BE bread for others?

   I get out the big bowl,
   measure out the ingredients:
   salt, sugar, shortening, water, flour, yeast.
   Stir it up, turn out on the board, knead,
   push, pull, slap, punch, shape, mold, cover,
   let rise in warm place.

The Gospels give me the ingredients for my life:
grains of wheat, salt of the earth, living water, leaven.
   God, knead me, mold me, shape me, form me,
   wrap me in the warm blanket of your love
   and let me grow
   so that I may bring bread to others,
   so that I may feed others with my life.

Give us this day our daily bread . . .

   Toast for breakfast, donut at coffee break,
   sandwich for lunch, warm dinner rolls
   dripping with butter.
   Millions of your children, God,
   my brothers and sisters,
   go to bed hungry each night.
   They lack even a crust of bread.
   What can I do to feed them?

Millions of your people do not have daily bread,
and they will surely die.
Millions of your people do not eat of the
bread of life—the Body of Christ—
and they too will surely die.
God, open my eyes to their needs
so that I may feed them—
not only their bodies,
but their souls as well.

Feed my lambs, feed my sheep . . .

   The bread comes from the oven,
   fragrant and warm.
   Its aroma fills the house,
   and passersby say,
   "Mmm, someone's baking bread."
   After it has cooled a bit,
   I wrap it gently and take it
   to the new neighbors.
   "Welcome to your new home.
   What can I do to help you?"

"The Body of Christ, Mary."
"The Body of Christ, Bill."
"The Body of Christ, Joe."
"The Body of Christ, Nancy."
Feed my lambs, feed my sheep . . .
How can I feed others when I am hungry?
Oh, Supreme Baker, lead me to your table often—
daily—that I may be nourished
with the Body of your Son, Jesus Christ.
Only then can I feed others.
I ask this in the name of Jesus
who is the holiest of bread.
Amen.

Ruth Kulas

Two Prayers: Martha and Mary

Martha

In this stewpot of a world
I intend to brew nourishment;
why rebuke me for furiously feeding
even you? even yours?

O Jesus, in my Martha heart
love breaks forth, a clamor
of pots and pans, of claims and causes,
insisting, insisting that I serve.

I would be quiet if I could,
but I seem called to bake and weave;
I would be shamed to leave you
naked and hungry as you teach!

Distracted though I can be,
my spirit bends to your words—
what more is this you ask of me?

Mary

What men think!
Unbinding my hair,
I am disgraced in their eyes.
Unbinding my hair,
I feel grace in your gaze.

As this oil epitomizes
earth's riches,
its fragrance ascending to heaven,
so you, my Friend,
are my life's treasure,
so your royal spirit lifts me up.

If I can afford your Being
pleasure and honor,
no risk is too great—
you have taught me that,
and it has set me free.

As I kneel at your feet,
I receive your blessing;
as I anoint you with this oil,
it becomes a river
of your love.

Though you suffer
a cross of fire,
give me courage to be with you.
The waters of Paradise
heal all wounds.

Nancy Corson Carter

Dried Beans, Bread, and Wine

Practice hospitality.

Romans 12:13, RSV

Two events in my life sum up one of the most important challenges I face as a Christian woman. The first took place in my Jesus-freak days in the 1970s. I belonged to a small community of single people who met for dinner and prayer on Friday nights. At some point we realized that just a few of us were taking responsibility for preparing dinner, and someone suggested that we might have potluck suppers in the future to spread the work around more evenly. We all agreed to bring something the following week.

The next Friday night when the food was placed on the table, we had a salad, a casserole, soda pop, and an unopened bag of dried beans. The beans were the contribution of three single men who shared an apartment. They were unable to understand why this was not a reasonable contribution to a potluck supper.

The second event happened more recently at Mass on Holy Thursday as I listened to the homily. The priest must have said "Jesus and his twelve Apostles" at least twenty times. I finally leaned over and whispered to a friend, "If it was only Jesus and his twelve Apostles, who made dinner?" She whispered back, "That's why they only had bread and wine."

The fact is that for the last two thousand years of Christianity, women have made the dinners, women have organized the potlucks and the coffee hours, women have set up the child care, and women have decorated the church. *And* we have gone completely unnoticed while doing these tasks. We do them so well and so invisibly that men don't even really know how they're done.

Those of us who have been reading feminist literature since the 1970s know why this is. It is because women's labor is undervalued. We women of the 1980s and 1990s have been determined that our labor not be undervalued. We are proving that we can be ministers, theologians, pastoral counselors, and church administrators. Meanwhile, who is making dinner?

Someone out there is thinking about Martha. When Martha worried about who was making dinner, Jesus told her that she should be like her sister, who was sitting around listening to the word of God. Whatever Jesus meant by this remark, I do not think that he meant he didn't want dinner. And if he was offering to go hungry so that Martha could sit with Mary and listen, I don't think it would have been easy to convince the disciples who were with him to give up their dinners also.

People do not hear the Gospel well on empty stomachs. Churches without child care lose members who have small children. It is impossible to build community without having people eat together.

As we Christian women of the 1990s assume a broader role in the church, we have to pay attention to who is making dinner. And if we want to eat something besides dried beans and bread and wine, we have to do more than suggest that the men help out in the kitchen. We have to teach them what to do, and we have to teach them why hospitality is an important ministry in the church.

So let the challenge for Christian women in the 1990s not be making women priests, but empowering men to organize a potluck supper where everyone gets enough to eat.

Billie Aul

Exegesis; Hermeneutics

There's a thaw today,
and the Mormons are out
on the sidewalks
preaching their Great American
Religion. Nice
young men, clean and overshoed,
in pairs, neat blond
and brunette sets always
watching over one another.

Lapsed Catholics like me wonder
why always the voice of God
is male. Never fresh-faced, smart
and female. I get introspective
and a little crazy when I'm bleeding.
I suppose therein lies the explanation:
women's hormones rage, distract
us from orderly passionate faith.
Self-pitying, I think about my daughters.

If they knock on my door, I plan to tell
these earnest, disciplined apostles
that they couldn't have picked a worse time:
I was just speaking in tongues to a friend
of mine who is about to fly
to the Balkans to view some Communist
children who claim to see the
Blessed Virgin—she expects (my friend)
to see her too; she is utterly
open to the Spirit, but we use the telephone
in honor of the social conventions.

Young men, I mean to ask them,
I know it's written down, but still,
how can you be so certain
that a woman's only way to heaven
is to marry? What potency is this
for a man to claim? My daughters
aren't at home just now, but
I intend to wave Rosie's bra,
Sarah's salty panties, Annie's
bowtie and suspenders—these banners—
over me: I have not just fallen away,
I have been justified by a female faith
alone. Through the lace curtains
I dare them to ring my bell.

Elizabeth Mische John

Pearls

To women aware in male institutions.

You are pearls:
you began
as irritants.

The ocean pushed
your small, nearly
invisible
rough body
through an undetected
crack in the shell.
You got inside.

Happy to have a home
at last
you grew close to the host,
nuzzling up
to the larger body.

You became a subject
for diagnosis:
invader, tumor.

Perhaps your parents
were the true invaders
and you were born
in the shell—
no difference—
called an outsider
still.

You were a representative
of the whole
outside world,
a grain of sand,
particle of the universe,
part of earth.
You were a *growth*.

And you did not go away.

In time
you grew
so large,
an internal
luminescence,

that the shell
could contain
neither you nor itself,
and because of you
the shell opened itself
to the world.

Then your beauty
was seen
and prized,

your variety valued:
precious, precious,
a hard bubble of light:
silver, white, ivory,
or baroque.

If you are a specially
irregular and rough
pearl, named baroque
(for broke),
then you reveal
in your own
amazed/amazing
body of light
all the colors
of the universe.

Alla Renée Bozarth

I Want New Saints

I want new saints
   saints with birch-tree souls
      whose leaves turn color and fall
         whose cruel winters freeze their
         naked branches.

I want saints with sunrise eyes
   whose Springs awaken sweat-sweet fertility,
   musk lusty,
      played out on sodden sheets,
         whose golden Summers bake
         their bodies brown.

I want angry saints
   with molten wills
      who squeeze their carbon hearts
      in rage and
         bring forth diamonds,
         weary saints,
            torn by countless beatings.

Saints who make
   extravagant mistakes
   and laugh,
      certain that, more than perfection,
      God desires truth.

Mary A. Bowen

The Next Poem

Your poems start out all right, but then they all have this sad little twist.
Sarah Elizabeth John

Have it be something happy,
something with dancing and singing and purple
wrapping, silver ribbons, winter stars
caught in the branches of some tree—
not an elm, this time.
Tell it this way: the manger was not
an ordinary cold cradle, the shepherds
not bad musicians or unkempt boors
confused by too much wine
and panic at the new taxes
demanded by Rome.

None of their wings were broken; not a single
angel was blind. There were women
reading in the temple, fascinated by birth
and not dull virginity. Try a real epiphany,
God shown forth in all Her creation:
and none of them carrying swords, and none
hungry at night
or hiding in the shrubs along reactionary roads.

Try it again, without irony and without
fatigue; be fearless in this dangerous place
where Grace is precious and slippery, a violet
in glacial latitudes; a grain of sand sliding
through eternity's bright sieve, a small
scar carved in the palm of Her hand.

Elizabeth Mische John

~

God of Worry and Fulfillment,
   Just as babies tend to be born
      when women's bodies are about to burst,
   Just as snow snaps off the fir tree
      when its weight is almost-too-much,
   Just as many people die
      when they have completed living,
So do I expect that this burden will lift,
if I wait actively just-long-enough.
   Just as You feed and nurture
      the fetus and women's bodies,
   Just as You help to create
      the snow and the fir tree,
   Just as You are God of Life and Death,
So I trust You to guide me to endure with meaning,
to wait expectantly, but not to wait too long.
   I accept the waiting,
      but hold fast to the vision of new birth.
   I drop excess weight,
      keeping only that of redemptive struggle.
   I am ready to let go of the burden—
      no need to cling to it fiercely.
Hopeful and weary,
   I co-operate with You,
God of Worry and Fulfillment.

Carolyn Stahl Bohler

Insight

I saw another facet of myself.
The awareness cut through my gut like lightning,
Left a tinge of nausea in my bloodstream.
A piece of my perfect dream,
Created with dash and style,
Traded once again for reality,
And the commission to love
Unconditionally,
This aging clump of clay.

Mary Hugh McGowen, OSB

Wouldn't It Be Horrible?

I resisted it all along,
Praying and pleading with God and you.
(You were always the father, leader, shepherd.)
I set out to fix the faults for you, me, them.
   Do you remember when we would
   lie in bed, summarizing the evening
   of friends' chatter about who's buying
   the house or the next baby on the way,
   and always came the murmurings of pain
   and separation, custody fights, visitation
   schedules? We would lie together and say,
   "Wouldn't it be horrible? It would be
   the worst. Never. Never."
And now the judge, faceless to me, has signed our papers.
The children will fly to visit you soon.
Your checks arrive by the fifth.
I check the marital status box "D."
I resisted it all along,
Praying and pleading with God and you,
But now, now that it's done,
I'm learning.
I'm strong enough to look my twelve-year-old in the eye and say "No."
I'm fair enough to catch a glance now and then.
I'm wise enough to hold a career with promise.
I have choices I never anticipated,
Time to think,
Energy to write,
A wrinkling of the surface with joy, ever so slight.
Within this death,
Life stubbornly pushes out.
With surprise, I laugh aloud.

Elizabeth Alexander

When I was young—a child, a teenager—I was my mother's confessor, the recipient of her mid-life regrets, the vessel of her second chance. I was born years after her third child, when she thought that she was done with diapers and drool, perhaps when she thought that she might be within a few years of making a break for it. While I do not wish to take back my existence, I think I knew early on that I was in the ambivalent position of being both a comfort and yet another sign of limit in my mother's world.

I heard her admissions of things that she would have done differently, given the chance, when my brothers and sister were small. She talked of being overwhelmed sometimes with their collective energy, of hasty punishments meted out in anger, of guilt over rupturing some unspoken maternal oath of trust and care by acts of utter frustration. At other times she would speak of her own father, an alcoholic, who would cheerfully give permission for an outing to his children while sober, only to withdraw the privilege violently and capriciously when drunk. I don't know if telling me, the innocent latecomer, relieved either her guilt or her own lingering childhood pain. It left me, at my kindest, wanting to treat her as a fragile thing, to shelter her as though she were the child (although I see now that she had survived much and was in her way very strong). At my teenage worst, I lashed out as only a teenager can, striking for the tender spots she had shown me.

I watched her as mother to my now-grown siblings, watched their often-terse exchanges, watched how moats of frustration and anger and disappointment opened up between them. I was not so much younger that I did not know my older brothers and sister at all. I was devoted to them, almost idolized them at times. I would watch them with our mother and feel my love stretched across those moats, twined among them all but strained by the distance between.

My mother died of cancer when I was not quite eighteen, in an ending that allowed enough time for reconciliation between her and her children, for direct confessions and forgiveness. By the time it was my turn to arrive at her bedside, there was no need for me to mediate, or try to smooth rough edges, or to hear last confessions. There was just the anguished grace of seeing someone in true peace with herself for the first time, even as it was time to say good-bye.

I have had to make my way into being an adult daughter without the woman who made me a daughter in the first place. I turn to her as example, warning, safe harbor, teacher, prickly thorn in my side, all in the abstract. Now, with the first deep roots of understanding that come from being a woman rather than a child, I summon her up from memory and reminiscence, searching for answers to questions I never knew to ask when she was still here in body. For a long time I started with my last moments with her, moving back and forth in time from that point, gliding on the grace that flowed from it, retroactively binding up wounds a generation back, gathering up the redeemed fragments of a family's history. It was a good place to start and a place to which I return.

But now I also go back to my mother, in memory, even before my memory, and try to look at her hurts and hurting without blinking, without the confessor's blind, anonymous screen. I look with anger, and I look with tears in my eyes; I look with the knowledge that if my birth set limits to who she might have been, her being my mother set limits to who I might be. We danced in a pattern defined by hurt and insecurity and love, according to seemingly indelible footsteps painted out by people long gone. I look with the slow, terrifying, life-giving knowledge that behind the peace and wholeness in my mother's eyes was a call to me not to wait until I was dying to claim life.

Julie Polter

Five Decades of Mary

When did we pass, sister?

When did we pass, Mary my mother,
Figure of my childhood formed
Of ambiguity and disheartened gaze—
Too restraining, too present, too imperious
For my eight-year-old child-playing heart.

Remember you my seventh-grade
Jealousy of your God-chosenness:
Why you and not me?
(I have become the Elizabeth of your
Annunciation days.)

Oh, my Mother and my Sister, too much
for my childhood. My oppressor, my competition—
I left you healthily on the shelf.

And began again at twenty to
Rethink you, my sister-self, hearing the
Word of God and keeping it.
Attentive to angel words, vital in
Visitation. Modest only to shield the
Adventuresome Mystery.

The girl for God, the woman for us.
In whom are hid the mystery of divinity and
right—alive!—humanity.
My companion, my cohort of those years—engaged,
Divinity enmeshed

Nazareth-homed, Bethlehem-journeyed, Jerusalem-bound
Late did I love you, my sister-soul,
Blessed among women.

And now I approach you, menopaused as I am,
Blood-spent as I am.
And find you once more, maybe.
Mother of this very old, finally, child.
Wondering at virginity—maybe now I know, maybe not, this
wedding with divinity.
This living oneself in feminine history, many decades now
related to the Wordmystery—
I know the cross. Blood always poured out, humanity always
mediating. Something's done in this, Mary.
A chosen past, split from the present by given fertility.

Different, you and I. I never had a Joseph, companion and
protector.
But mothered I have; God-wed I've been—a shaky marriage,
that.
And now Sister, Mother Mary, Virgin Girl of Nazareth,
Genatrix of the Divine and most Human One,
I come—ambiguity surpassed, beyond shared years.

I see you again, young girl, and
Find myself strangely the
Elizabeth for your Annunciations.

Rosemary Broughton

Trusted

The woman caught
between the well that
answers thirst and
the well that waters life
did not know how
to change until
Jesus trusted her
as one who knew.

The woman caught
between the stones of
angry men accusing with
their epithets
did not have the energy
for change until
Jesus trusted her as
one who knew what
was best for her.

The woman whose blood would not cease its flow
until she trusted that
in touching him
it did not matter that
he knew or did not know—
in touching him
she trusted that she knew.

Kathryn Cramer Brown

Tiller of Life

For years I crewed.
You sailed,
knowing well the wind in ways
that yet escape me:
when to trim the sail or let it out,
how to catch a breeze just beyond
the boat, to let out before
a gust and reef before
a squall—to tack and
return home almost on time.

I packed picnics and remembered children's toys,
knew the jib, but not the main,
read novels on the bow.
Slicing through the summer daze
mooring for a dip—
it was a kind of ecstasy,
the water and the wind.

The cold winter of your death
brought harsh realities.
Shovel out the driveway
before I go to work.

Pay the orthodontists.
Raise children on my own.
The sleet and snow
hung deep that year.
I learned to be alone.

Then in early spring
your voice awakened me.
"Sail the boat yourself," it said,
"Don't sell it yet until you try."
In the clarity of coffee
I called the boatyard man:
"I've changed my mind.
Don't sell it yet. I'll want
it there in June."

Skimming on the water
over oceanic fears—
I proved myself and returned
relieved to dock and rest.
To sell the boat, to wait, to heal,
and to forget the wind.

But now
Years later in a smaller boat
No beauty on the bow—
I shift my weight and hike it out
Capsize and sometimes cry.

There's a different splendor to it—
Different, but bold.
Back and forth
Wind and water
Wind and
me.

Nancy Fitzgerald

Words Like Flowers

I am in the sixth year after my husband, Pat, died, and I am healing.
Ann asks how long it takes. I don't want to say forever, although I
sometimes think it will take forever, as an image rises out of the past

of blood or loneliness or sitting by the stereo in my recliner, unable to move, unable to listen to the voices of Marie and Kathy and Gendren, who have come to comfort me. I sit in my recliner and listen to "Kali's Dream," music that has not the specificity of words and so can wash the pain away with sound.

It is now the sixth year. Ann wants to know how long. She has tears in her eyes. Her eyes are black, large, tender, wet, and shining. Her mother is dead only two or three months, and she wants to know how long.

After two months, John, who had loved me twenty-seven years, came to me and laid healing hands on my body, my flesh, flayed with whips. John's hands felt warm, heavy, able to form the flesh like moist clay. Able to fire me like a pot in a kiln—later like a beautiful vase, a blue vase with green and silver all melding together, shining, translucent. Clay that emits light.

I rested. I lay in bed till sunset and rose to eat omelets, which John fixed with olives and cheese, smothered in white mounds of sour cream, heaped with bacon. I had lost flesh. You could feel my bones. John built new flesh for me with food. He kissed me to hold it in place. He smothered my flesh with his hand. He said, "Live." He said, "I love you. I love you forever." John married me again to life.

John took me into the hills. We walked among trees. We sat in vines looping down from branches, clinging tenaciously so I would not fall. John swung the vine, and I floated, feet off the ground, sky in my eyes, the leaves like flowers floating over me.

John took me to the ocean. Half Moon Bay. We played with waves. We made love on the sand, hidden by cliffs, protected by the wind. We made love in waves of healing that washed over us—because by this time the pain in each of us had married, and the healing became mutual. We walked the beach. We bent and picked up shells, stones, small feathers of gulls. John clasped love around me like a necklace. It is a gull with reaching wings. The Eternal Spirit in a flight of gold.

I began to write. I found words for poems, for prayers, for books. I lived in words. I built a house of words. Around the corners of my house I stacked words like flowers. Daisies, roses, chrysanthemums. I grew bleeding hearts. I watered them. I made windows for sunlight and hung lace curtains. The sun filtered through lace. Cast images on my walls. Made dreams. I rested in dreams of light and flowers. I kissed each of my fingers and set them on the keys. I made words and healed.

Christin Lore Weber

Six-Oh!

This year's gone. What have I to show for it?
They argue that the decade includes the aught.
But my safe fifties now are done. I ought
to grieve, for where's my job, my call? I fit
no pattern I had hoped to find. I thought
with gifts, experience from age, I'd do
church ministry, but when that door slammed to
(crunched toes!), I learned God's will includes the not.
Now, as the Nineties dawn, they look to Two-
oh-oh-oh, longing for a kinder world,
a new beginning. Oh, but six-oh hurled
no promise. None for gifts untried, unused.
God smiles at this late insight. "Now you see
you're free to speak, to write. Begin. For me."

Elizabeth A. Moore

Widow's Well

I went away today
And took along my cup,
So empty that
It ached and sagged
With need to fill it up.

I visited my well,
And dipped it to the brim.
All old and dear
But fresh and clear
With memories of him.

I raised it to my lips
And drained it down with zest.
With joys gone by
To cheer me, I
Can handle all the rest.

I stayed to drink my fill
And felt my spirit soar
My yearning fell
And lo, the well
Was full as just before.

I rested till the well
Reflected back my smile
The healing mood
Of gratitude
Washed over me awhile.

You're welcome to my well.
Come keep me company.
The one no doubt to talk about
I'd really like is he.

He'd love to know you'd come.
So smile and lift a toast
Drink all you please
Of memories,
My husband is the host.

Jean M. Wood

Southern Awakening

I was raised a Southern Belle, she spoke
in gentle words, so soft a voice,
and God made man to care for me
to think my thoughts
speak my words
so I could be a lady, free
unhampered by the devious world
of making decisions, living my life.

At forty-six I learned, she spoke
in a firm, still-gentle woman's voice,
in God's image we were made
both man and womankind
and man, not God, set limits
on my life. Don't quote Paul to me.
Did Paul tell Lydia, dealer
in purple cloth—to royalty?
(It could be—):

> Go home to your family.
> Give up this crazy idea of being
> a businesswoman.

No. He baptized Lydia, broke bread,
and blessed her household. Paul knew.
God knew that women
had work to do. Brains and plans
and prayers too big to conceal
in white kid gloves and picture hats.

Lois Oller Nasados

Prayer

Our soul mate,
Who is ever within and without,
Holy is your name.

Let us live with you;
Be our perceptions and responses.
Let us be in unity, now and forever.

Give us this day what we truly need.
Forgive us our faults as we forgive
The shortcomings of others.

Lead us always to wholeness.
Protect and love us forever.

For yours is everything.
Everything that is even the
Least bit good
Leads directly to you.

Amen.

Andrea Cook Cockrell

Part 4

For all these mysteries—
for the wonder of myself,
for the wonder of your works—
I thank you.

Psalm 139:14, *Psalms Anew*

Who Am i Before God?

i am—a pebble, being kicked along a
        path by a small child.
but, at times, a boulder—immense, immovable

        a raindrop, dripping off the roof,
        splashing on someone's head.
        a flood, my waters raging—
        thundering over the shores.

i am—a seedling, weak, but strong enough
        to stand against nature.
    a giant oak tree, my trunk twisted with age,
    showing the scars of years gone by.

        i am a fenced-in lot, allowing some in,
        keeping others out.
        an open field, grass swaying in the breeze,
        laughter, swings, and a sandbox.
                no fences.

Mary E. Taylor

1968

Tonight I remember suddenly
From so long ago
Like a dream forgotten then recalled
How she brushed her guitar gently
And sang out of all the struggles of the years,
"Precious Lord, take my hand. . . ."
In the dark night of black and white hatred
Darkness of my unbelief
At deep dark on a summer evening
I sat safe and green on her Campbell Street porch
When no one else was talking to the likes of me.
She dared to love me anyway,
And her husky voice
Hanging on the darkness
"Precious Lord . . ."
Made a believer of me.

Sue B. Ralph

The Choice

The pain remained in her eyes as she spoke. I prayed that it would flow from her eyes with the tears, but it was much too deep. As she told me why she had made the choice, my heart went out to her. The reason seemed so right and justified. She had made the choice, as others have, and now the pain of the choice lives with her, haunts her, never letting her forget. She can never go back and change the past.

The "choice" had also been presented to me. It seems so long ago now, but one never forgets. I was a young sixteen, longing to be an adult. I looked like most sixteen-year-olds of that time and place: long hair parted in the middle, T-shirt, bell-bottomed, hip-hugger jeans. I was sure that being an adult would be so easy. Of course, I believed my parents did not understand how really grown up I was. I was mature, but they just didn't recognize it. Love, as I knew it then, consumed me. He was my whole life, and I had to show him how much I really loved him.

In a borrowed car on an early warm July morning, I drove myself to the clinic. I was not feeling at all well that morning, and I knew why. I didn't really need to go to the clinic for the answer. The heavyset nurse, full of compassion for the child sitting across the desk, told me the results of the test. I was pregnant.

There was no joy in my heart at that moment, just fear. It totally consumed me: how my parents would be hurt, angry, disappointed. Would my boyfriend still love me? How would I finish high school? No college for me. What was I going to do?

The nurse laid her hand on my hand, and with great compassion and concern for the decision that would affect the rest of my life, she presented me with the "choice."

"You know, you can have an abortion."

The room swirled around me.

Was I brave? Was I stupid? Was I a good Catholic? Was it the way I was raised? Was I naive? Was it just another challenge to show everyone I was grown up? I'm not sure. But within minutes of the truth of knowing I was to have a child, I loved that child. I made the choice and stuck by it for the rest of my life.

The years were full of good, but not easy, times. I ignored the freshmen who stared at the pregnant senior. I wore my wedding dress to my prom. I found a babysitter for my high school graduation. But I was also gifted with seeing my little girl's first steps, with receiving her first "thank you," with hearing her first word—"bear." The list of hard times could go on, but so could the list of gifts.

I do wonder at times if the child held me back from making more of myself. Or is it possible that the child motivated me to the point of being something even better, the person I am today?

The impact of my long-ago choice wanders through my mind in quiet moments of reflection. I remember the painful words of friends who chose abortion. May God's loving grace touch their hearts and ease their pain. I recall the words so easily spoken by the compassionate nurse that long-ago July morning. I feel the pain of the sacrifices made over years of struggling to raise a child and grow up too. I close my eyes and ponder the choice. Was it the right choice? Then, in my reflection, I see the person who has touched my heart, who has shared my tears, joys, and love, and I can only thank God for the choice I made and for my daughter.

Jocelyne Askins

Heart Flower

Sweet Flower of youth's untimely passion,
budding in some hidden realm,
unknown by root or stock,
claimed by foreign hands and
grafted onto another genealogy.

I look for your fervent brown eyes in
children in the streets and
magazine photographs. The
black hair that blazes in the sun
like raven's wings, the skin of
creamy softness.

We name you "the Hidden Rose"
and cherish your existence
from afar. Gift—given in
tears and brought at great
price.

Loved in sorrow and
pain—you are loved by
hearts that never saw your
smile and longed for by
hands that never held you.

Remember, our love for you was
greater than our selfish desire
of possession . . . so we yielded
you to other arms and other
hearts.

But know that on the journey
of life, the road you walk
was given in love,
and our love is forever with you.

You are the hidden rose,
and a rose is just as sweet by
any other name. . . .

Oneata Harrigan

One Crisp Morning

One crisp morning a woman came to me dressed in God-knows-what
    and an attitude of splendor.
I invited her in for tea
    and for hours she whispered delicious tales.
She said she saw me dance once—
    in the shadowy basement of my house.
Seemingly, I blushed—
    remembering the joyful tears and aching laughter of
    myself thinking I was alone.
She said she saw me cry once—
    in the bathroom of a friend's house.
Seemingly, I blushed—
    remembering the pounding fists and weeping sounds of
    myself thinking I was alone.
She said she often saw me sleep—
    and I always invited an angel in for tea.
Seemingly, I blushed—
    finally realizing it was She.

Kerry B. Danner

Living in the Womb of God

I've always treasured 2:00 a.m. feedings. It seemed to be the only time that I got to hold my baby without having to divide my time between the other children. In the middle of the night, the two-year-old that was always eager to plant sticky peanut-butter kisses on the nursing baby was now sound asleep, scrubbed squeaky clean and tucked between fresh sheets. The four-year-old who always brought me his favorite book at precisely the same moment that the baby needed to be fed was now safe and sound asleep in dreams, with his books scattered on the floor all around him. Even my considerate husband, who shared with me all the details of his business transactions of the day, was now making sounds of contented, deep sleep. And so I am alone with our baby. This is my time to recapture the intimacy we shared when only I knew the inner stirrings of the child nestled deep within my womb. Now this precious infant belongs to everyone, and I must claim my intimate moments at two o'clock in the morning.

One night as I sat in the dark of my living room holding the baby that had fallen asleep at my breast, I marveled at the gift of life. This gift of life *given to me*. This child, so fragile, so dependent, is loved unconditionally simply because he exists. He grew in my womb and was brought forth in living water, making me so vulnerable, making me see life brand new all over again. I know that if a hair were brushed to the wrong side, I would know it. If he were to get hurt I would feel the pain. To love so much is to allow myself to be unbelievably vulnerable.

Somewhere in my wonderings at 2:00 a.m., I began a dialog with God. I knew in my head that God's love was even more perfect than mine, but I couldn't understand it in my heart. How could there be a more perfect love than that of parents for their child? Two o'clock became a sacramental moment, for I was able to see that the child asleep in my lap was a perfect container for God's love. To look at the face of God and know God's love would be too awesome for me to handle. In the image of my child I could safely encounter the unconditional love of God.

The early morning feeding and the baby became the sacred time and place in which I could connect with God. At some point I became acutely aware of God's love enveloping me. I became the baby lying in the lap of God. I felt the presence of a God who feels my pain and counts the hairs on my head. I was aware of being intimately connected to God, my Creator. The union was as intimate as the connection between me and the child that grew in my womb. In the dark of my living room I knew what it was like to live in the womb of God. I felt the nurturing power of God's love pulsing through me. I knew that the source of all of my love was God. At the 2:00 a.m. feeding, I was being fed. Sometime between the dark of night and the light of day I was called by name, and I came to know what it means to be a daughter of God.

Karen DeFilippis

God, Our Nursing Mother

So that you may be suckled and satisfied
from her consoling breast,
so that you may drink deep with delight
from her generous nipple. . . .
You will be suckled, carried on her hip
and fondled in her lap.
As a mother comforts a child,
so I shall comfort you. . . .

Isaiah 66:11–13, NJB

Mother God,
I lie close to you, my head on your breast.
I drink deeply from your generous nipple.
I drink in stars, planets, whirling galaxies,
your infinite night.
You take me on journeys beyond my imaginings,
tell me wonderful stories in strange languages
that I somehow understand.
Overwhelmed, I watch your mouth form
love poems and songs for me.
Then, bold with tenderness,
I dare to touch your lips with my fingertips.

My tears remind me of my ecstatic delight.
The scent of wild roses surrounding us
returns me to this wooded place.
As I lie content in your embrace,
"like a weaned child in her mother's arms,"
I hear the nearby waterfall splashing in its pool.
You carry me there and hold me up in the water,
sun shining on my nakedness.
With your comforting touch
my tense shoulders relax
and release their old burdens into the water.
As your hand massages my taut neck muscles,
memories—images of childhood wounds—
rise to the surface in these healing waters.
I release them into your hands.
You send them, small minnows, down the stream
into the ocean of your forgiveness.

You let me float on my own now, savoring my freedom.
I lean myself back into the water.
I am held by it, opened by it.
I feel your presence
> in the water
> in the sun
> in me
And
> I
>> float
>>> free

Barbara Blake, RSM

In the Night

The night is thick around me.
Bradford's hand rests heavily on my shoulder.
I stroke his hand
And run my fingers through his baby-fine hair.
More than half-asleep, I prolong this moment—
This time of baby snug against my breast.
The air fills with our breathing.
Gathered with me I feel in spirit
The presence of my mother and grandmother.
I ache that they will never hold
This sweet child of mine.
And yet I feel their arms around the two of us.
In the dark I whisper
Tales of smiling and cooing.
Stories of first crawling and pulling up.
First a chuckle, then a tear:
In spirit and in flesh,
We the generations of motherhood
Hold this child,
Cherishing his life and dreaming of his future.

MaryJane Pierce Norton

Tonight I Was Remembering

The sun was low in the sky and calling me to times past.
It was chore time and I looked out of the kitchen window.
The lilacs were small then and so were you. They were
Laced delicately with tiny green leaves and the hint of fragrance
    yet to come.

It was spring and the chickens were busy, and as you emerged
From the lilac stand, your eyes were round and large
Carrying the treasures from the nests, in your basket.
Even Sea Shell had gifted you with a tiny egg.

You wore jeans and little red sneakers, a white shirt
Busy with the signs of an active day. But I remember
Most, the red bandana that covered your long dark hair,
The knot tied under your chin.
I knew then that there was much fragrance
    yet to come.

Annamarie Burtness

Preserve

The cellar shelf in dimness baits my eyes.
A long-forgotten jar of jam at last
I find and bring forth like a prize.
The dusty label's date was three years past.

Held up, the windowlight gleams softly through
Red berries ripe the summer he was three.
My baby girl was two days overdue.
I smiled back as the neighbors laughed to see
Me take my basket and my little son
To show him where the sweetest berries grew
In wild profusion, showed him how to pick
The ones just ripe. And then he watched me brew
The fragrant scarlet sweetness to preserve.

I try to think how further went the day.
Still warm and sliding on a buttered crust
He sampled some before he went to play.

We two together partied in the shade.
I swabbed his mouth and fingers, watched him go
And turned to glow with windowsills of jars
Once more before I took them down below.

Now three years hence, the three of us are here
To try the spread again beneath the tree.
His hands, no longer small, so surely hold
The sandwich while my baby on my knee
Too soon jumps down. Both run away. The jam
Is still as sweet and bright: But though I try
I can't remember quite how he was then,
Just how he walked and talked with shining eye.

Oh, mothers everywhere, before too late,
I beg you to discover yet a way
The sweetness of a child's each smile and look
May be preserved to sample on a day

When they are gone.

Jean M. Wood

Thoughts on Motherhood

I laughingly call them "the Vikings"—these blond, blue-eyed boys who are my sons. Like Viking hoards, they are constantly ready to sweep down upon the house to plunder and pillage their surroundings. They have an uncanny way of knowing the exact moment I have been able to bring some measure of order to the house.

I am in awe of the power of their presence in my life. I suppose that I always thought a mother and child would be more in tune—more a part of each other. They are of my body and soul, and yet so separate from me. I often look at them as they play or sleep, and I wonder, "Who are these people? And what part am I to play in their growing up and becoming?"

Austin and Jordan—by naming them, I somehow make them more my own. Yet in my heart I know that they are part of the very energy of life—mine only for a while—belonging truly to the Creator of all life and put here for God's purpose.

Mary must have felt this way—awe, wonder, separateness—as she watched her son lying in the manger so long ago.

Deborah B. Sims

God, He Went to School Crying Today

We forgot to practice the spelling words until the last minute.
He could not get *laugh*.
He kept forgetting the *u*.
I made him write it five times.
I did not notice that he had not finished his cereal.
Some milk spilled on his favorite shirt.
"Do you want to change your clothes?" I asked.
"No, I will just tuck it in," he answered.
At that very moment we heard the bus' brakes
screech as it rumbled round the corner.
"Do you have everything—shoes, backpack, lunchbox?"
He had everything, except the *u* in *laugh*.
God, put the *u* in *laugh* for him.
Help this rough-and-tumble start not color his
whole day melancholy gray.
Send someone to give him extra love today, when I
cannot reach him.
Do a little transforming in my boy, too.
Help him learn to work through tears toward smiles
and maybe even laughs.

Sharon Kerr

Isn't That What Life Is All About?

The rain fell softly—just enough to water the bright green grass and keep the boys inside. They were playing a record, drumming, and playing the guitar in accompaniment, creating a high-decibel din. Then—joy—the rain stopped, and they could go outside. Solitude. I could get some work done.

Rounding up the boys' missing mittens and heavy jackets took ten minutes. I refused to hunt for their rain boots. I ushered them out the back door to play with the dog.

Back to my personal computer. Now, which story do I need to rewrite?

The back door opened. "We're too hot with these mittens on, Mom," the boys chorused as they threw the mittens in. The cat pounced on the mittens like a flash, threw them in the air, and batted them around the room.

Books about writing called to me. Stories waited to be written.

The back door opened. Number-one son's voice pierced the air: "He hit me!" Number-two son yelled, "He hit me first!" Out to the back yard I went to settle the fray.

Number-three son followed me in, wanting a drink. Five minutes later, out he went. An imitation smile adorned my face as I propelled him out the door.

I breathed a grateful sigh as I headed toward my computer. Which story do I rewrite? "Come on, remember what you learned from the correspondence course you just finished," I said out loud to myself.

The back door opened again. "Can we have some candy, Mom?" number-one son asked. I nearly shouted "No!" Then a light went on in my head. If they eat, they won't bother me for at least ten minutes, I thought. "Take three Snickers," I said. "No, take six—two for each of you." Aha, a candy overdose. He viewed me with disbelief as I handed him all six candy bars.

I rushed to my computer with glee and gave it a hug as I sat down to begin a story. If all went well, perhaps I could fold the laundry, start dinner, and salvage the day.

The back door opened. I sank my head into my hands and listened as six little feet patted toward me.

"Now what?" I asked.

"Mom, come practice football plays with us. You know, like we did in the den last week. We need more help on which way to run when the ball is snapped." He took my hand and pulled me out of my chair.

The serious appeal in his eyes did the trick. I shut the computer off, put on my jacket, and went out the back door.

"What we need, Mom, is you to give the plays in the huddle, then watch us to see if we go the way we are supposed to. Okay?"

I watched for a while, then of course I was running plays with them, huffing and puffing. The next thing I knew, I was on the bottom of the pile, yelling, "Get off me you big brutes!" Mistake! They started tickling me, and I tickled them. We were rolling around and around on the wet grass, laughing so hard tears were running down our cheeks.

There we all were, lying on our backs looking up at the sky. I knew my body would ache that night.

My books lay unread, my computer unused. The laundry was still unfolded. Yet, I knew the day had been liberated with giggling, candy, and fun. After all, isn't that what life is all about?

Connie Bedgood

The Crazy Quilt of Life

in the pattern of God's purpose
we are stitched together in caring and communion:
scraps of the lingering past,
fragments broken from future's dearest hopes;
textures of disappointment and dreams,
prints of pain and promise:
calico and corduroy,
stripes, silks, and satins—
all the colors of emotion and experience
are sewn
into a crazy quilt
of life,
patched together and transformed
into a blanket
of love . . .
and our compassion
comforts
a cold and hurting world.

Barbara Battin

Rhubarb

Like celery? a Brooklyn guest guesses
when I name the ovened dessert.

Stalky, stringy, juicy, otherwise
of little resemblance.
Spring's firstfruit boasts
of roots, indestructible as dandelion;
poisoned leaves, broad as burdock;
stems for cubing, sour as sin—
until stewed and sugared smooth as honey,
red and green as appleskin.
I offer in sauce dishes
the justified reeds, steaming,
caked with Mother's country dough,
and in the living room we taste and talk
of our pasts and presents, separated by
rivers wider than bridges.

I, too soon, swallow my last spoonful
of nostalgic delight.
She, too quietly, slips her full bowl
under the edge of her chair.

Evelyn Bence

Sacramental Deja Vu

We shop for a white-for-purity dress
in a size that surprises me. Still
I am unconvinced this child of peaches
and honey-spun-from-the-spoon
requires more than incidental grace.

Already this season the sun
has caught her; keeps vigil subsumed
in her cheeks, her brow, and her satin arms.
Her voice across the warm, still air
is Minnehaha's or a fishwife's.

I do not willingly make this daughter
a mock and premature bride; I will not
buy a veil, a net that does not suit her.
Instead we choose a wreath of dawny rosebuds
set in baby's breath and ribbons.

I've paid too much for her new underwear
and stockings—I want to give her comfort
where I was given starch. A cross, however
golden, is too macabre: instead, a pearl
grown in oyster flesh will hang about her neck.

Nine times or a dozen she practices the route
from vestibule to altar. Three freckled, sweaty
boys lure her with candles and cruciform
to one table she may not serve.
Her father says I have too little faith—this

may be so: scratched mothers show the pagan
through the surface sheen of gilt. In better worlds
the daughters all go barefoot, not pinched
in patent leather; thoughtlessly wear white in May;
go everywhere, dancing, with roses in their hair.

Elizabeth Mische John

Surfer

Through roiling water, cloudy with churned-up sand,
A girl in a slick wetsuit, prone on her board,
Breaks loose from a bobbing set of boys
And paddles out to distant undulations of the bay
To practice a sport seldom claimed by her kind.

On this early morning
Bright from glints of light off water
She lifts and dips toward outlying ridges,
Her head arched back,
Blonde braid sogged between her shoulders;

On top, within, under the heaving swells,
Taking her time to ply the creased water and read the waves,
She awaits the mysterious, precise moment. . . .

Presently she turns her board to shore
And pauses, letting an easy rise
Peak up to a smooth high hill;
At the appropriate time (she senses when)
She pushes herself erect, hands and feet thrusting,
And poses, ready as a bareback rider
To summon and control the problematic balance.

White froth forms on the breaker birthing across her path,
And tensed, alert,
She wills to conquer the in-moving sea.

Borne upward, her lithe body shines;
Sun-sparkles dart everywhere off her world
As she trims, juts forward, aslant on the angling breaker,
Straining to best its rage and its roar
Until the crested wall climaxes, curls, then plummets,
And her board, its fin unable to hold,
Wheels, throwing her into a sand-charged wake.

Once upright, she watches her wave die to a memory
of hissing effervescence splayed on the beach;
Then, subdued, she retrieves her skittering board. . . .
    Tonight, on her bed in a lull before sleep
    (Dry hair unbraided, flexed muscles recalling)
    She will review the pitch of perfection she sought

And plan that tomorrow
She will again stroke out to some newly spawned wave,
Again oppose the bay with all daring and desire;

And when sleep breaks over her
Perhaps she will dream of a heavenly world
Where she, blessed at last
With superior skill and tractable breakers,
Will catch a faultless wave
And perfectly surf toward an ideal shore,
Ecstatic, elated, rejoicing.

Marie Sagués, OP

Pat's Wedding-Day Smile

If you see my face blush today,
    it is because my mind is pleased—

Pleased with a man who is strong enough
    to pour out his earnest love
    yet soft enough to drink mine in;
Pleased with a man who is smart enough
    to work out his honest goal
    yet sure enough to spur mine on.

If you see my eyes mist today,
    it is because my heart is filled—

Filled with a man who is wise enough
    to blot out his foolish anger
    and kind enough to calm mine down;
Filled with a man who is brave enough
    to test out his newest idea
    and sweet enough to think mine through.

If you see my mouth smile today,
    it is because my life is blessed—

Blessed with a man who is frank enough
    to let out his inmost need
    yet free enough to hear mine out;
Blessed with a God who is keen enough
    to point out our freshest course
    and good enough to lift us up.

Cozette R. Garrett

One Woman's Response to an Earthquake

Mother Earth,
why do you quake and shudder
beneath my feet?
You groan with such a fury
I dare not think—
what will be born of such a labor?

Oh, when will you stop?
When will you cease shaking loose
all that I thought was firm and solid,
safe and secure?

They say there are shifts
in your chambers below,
causing movements
irregular, traumatic
and real.

It matters not if I am
awake or asleep,
indifferent or careful,
alarmed or serene
you will quake and shudder,
moan and groan under my feet,
adjusting to the changes
deep within your being.

A wooden doorframe
the safest place for me.
I stand on the threshold,
grounded in the present,
clinging to that which frames me,
a pillar to the left,
a pillar to the right.

I stand still
though I really want to run.
I stand on the threshold,
my back to the past.
I look to the future,
facing straight ahead.
My arms stretch out,
clutching the wood on either side.
My heart is spread open
in hope and fear.

Oh, my God!
Oh, my MaMa Earth!
There *is* a shift
in the chambers below.
You have midwifed
a change
deep within my being.

I leave my wooden doorframe
to be with another.
"May I sit with you awhile?"
I ask, trembling from within.
Communion is yearned for,
companionship sought.

"Where were you when the earthquake happened?"
we question one another.
I was on a threshold
hanging on to life!

Ann Perrin

The Magnificat of the Midwife

My soul proclaims the greatness and glory of God,
And my spirit exalts in God my Savior,
For God has permitted me to witness a holy birth,
The Christ Child come into the world.
When she who was chosen labored,
I was by her side.
I held her hand as she was seized by pangs of birth,
Assuring her that she was not alone,
And that this piercing pain would soon pass.
I witnessed the crowning, Glory be to God,
The moment new life emerged,
Speaking softly to ease the mother's fear and apprehension.
Helping to sever the cord, I raised the infant in my hands,
Wiped blood from his wriggling infant body,
And wrapped him tightly in soft cloth.
At that moment, I could have sworn that angels were singing,
And that the star-filled night shone on him alone.
Never will I forget that night—
That night when new life was born
So quietly, so gently, in a dung-filled stable.

Always will I remember
That the birth of the Holy
Comes in this way:
With pangs of labor,
With apprehension,
With blood and with tears,
Always giving way,
In due course,
As they did on this most wondrous of nights,
To hope,
To faith,
To love,
And to Life.

Judy Cannato

A Faithful Woman
(Proverbs 31:10–31 for the Nineties)

When one meets a faithful woman,
the moment is an awakening.

She has committed her heart to goodness,
and the world has an unfailing friend.

She develops her gifts with joy;
she empowers those around her.

She will dance in response to song;
she will grieve in response to pain.

She is decisive with wisdom and insight;
with compassion she makes her choice.

She knows she is wounded and needs healing;
she cannot do all things.

Life, for her, has purpose and pattern,
yet she bows before its mystery.

She is sometimes feared by men who meet her
until they discover and embrace
the woman within themselves.

Louise Marie Prochaska, SND

Everyday Parousia

Standing in line at Krogers,
I muse about the chances
Of Jesus showing up here
First, long before checking
Out a new foyer at my church.

Would he gaze at the
Astonishing beauty of a
Delicate young black girl
Whose brother tries to climb
Out of the cart while her
Mother buys milk with a WIC card.

Or would he touch the man
Leaning on a cane whose
Face is weary, comfort the
Old woman who pushes her
Cart as if it contained
A planetfull of pain.

On a day I perversely wound
Myself: "There's no one to
Rescue you. No one to watch over
You. No one will say, 'I'm sorry
For your pain.'"

And then he is there, a
Neighbor well into his eighties
Who thanks me for a dessert
I took by his house. (Out of
my largesse, was it a cup of water?)

He says, "Where are you on
Wednesday nights? I miss
Seeing you at church supper."

I load my groceries in the car
And breathe in gratitude for
A view of the second coming
In a parking lot.

Mary Zimmer

Suppertime

Compelled,
I went back to Anne Hutchinson
and the Antinomian Controversy.

And the rice burned.

She called me to come,
Witness her wisdom, and learn
Her defiant theology of grace.

And we picked up pizza.

Sister of mine in this battle to
Love God and dare honesty when
Men have silencing on their minds.

We went out for Chinese.

The wind blows hard out of a
Blue, blue sky. Spirit speaks to
The Governor: "I am poured out
Upon the Daughters and
They
Shall
Prophesy."

I start packing for Rhode Island.

Mary Zimmer

And Your Daughters Shall . . .

"Dad, the Body of Christ, the Bread of Heaven."

With those words I bent to place the Communion wafer into my father's hands during the Eucharist, which immediately followed the ordination to the diaconate of myself and two other candidates for Holy Orders.

With those words I looked him in the eyes, and both of us began to fill with tears. In those hectic years of being parent to five children, of which I was the fourth, could he ever have imagined such a moment, when I would be seeking to feed him a different kind of bread?

With those words my forty-five years of salvation history came that much closer to both its earthly and divine sources—a connection in which the daughters of man count, as well as the sons of man.

With those words we both were fed, and my "official" birth to a new stage in my developing life began.

Our family is hardworking, quite ordinary. I feel more at home in country chapels than in cities or cathedrals. Yet oddly, my new home is in a very urban setting; my current parish home is a cathedral.

"God," I whisper, "what an odd sense of humor you have. I'd never have come here but for so many tiny baby steps. I do wonder what you are about."

But wherever I am led from here, I will never forget that moment or the impact of my seventy-five-year-old father—source of half of my genetic pool (my mother is present among the heavenly multitude)—kneeling at the altar rail.

"Dad, the Body of Christ, the Bread of Heaven."

"Amen."

Elaine M. Silverstrim

Single White Female of the Cloth

"SWF
age 40
prot minister
seeks
smart
funny
man
with flair for romance"
is the way the ad in
the *New York Daily* reads

but she's not willing to risk job, life, or pregnancy
for premarital sex

well, what's a woman to do?

no sexual shenanigans and
saturday nites she's busy

also she must bury, marry,
and baptise during the week

the power she has is really
quite overwhelming but

keeps her on the up-and-up

because dates are easier to
come by, she says,
than church members
in her small congregation

some men say it feels like
kissing a nun

but life goes on under
the cloth

Helen G. Crosswait

Through-Hiker on the Appalachian Trail

Walking from Georgia to Maine,
I breathe out balsam
instead of air of airports
and manufactured smells of cars and carpeting.
The breeze never loses its new smell of morning.
The only rhythms are of boots and birds:
my walking and their alert songs.

At night I hear only my heart—
and unknown calls that I wish farther away, then closer.
During some nights without the moon,
I can see by the stars,
but sometimes
even
they
retreat.

In towns people feel suspicion and malice
toward someone with two thousand miles of leisure.
But in some post offices are women
who cherish the constant comfort of chatter
and are kind to anyone who must spend weeks
among living things that cannot speak.

The postmistresses give me packages of new boots
and letters for which I am most greedy—
not even walking away from the counter before I read.
My name in the address
seems an intimate offering,
those curved lines fine and human—
so unlike nature's;
even its twigs are ampler.
I think of the friend's hand that
smoothed along this envelope,
pocket it,
and then tear my name off a package to save it.

In a week without mirrors or bathing,
the only part of me that I have seen
is my hands, the growing nails
reminding me that I continue.
Sometimes I place the pure human color of my fingers
against sky
or tree
or soil
and touch fingers to each other,
trying to summon hands I have touched,
and the caresses that I thought
were in memory.
But I am here
to replace memory with exhaustion,
though every noise seems a contrast to laughter.

I look again and again
to these exposed mountains
that have yielded to sun and rain
and are serene.

I will become serene.

April Selley

Playground for Rocks
(Bangor, PA)

If God were a stone, God would live in this pasture.
The stones stand eight,
ten,
twelve feet high.
They seem to be trying
not to laugh.

From the chapel they looked indigent.
Only as I crossed the creek
and emerged from the darkening trees
could I see how tall they stood,
how thick the light.

They are engaged in standing still,
in letting the sun shine over them,
letting the voice of the man on the hill calling his dog
drift over them,
letting what is and what never will be
drift over them,
until sun and sound and eternity
are as much a part of the stone
as the stone.

Mary Cartledge-Hayes

The Braided Rug

I was never to know her children
I doubt that her daughter knew me
It wasn't her kinfolk in the house
That I would come to see

I'd hold off for an afternoon visit
To the room at the head of the stairs
They were not for us, the parlors,
With their stark and padded chairs

She'd respond to the chimes when I rang them
Then I'd follow her straight to the top
If ever she strayed to the front of the house
It wasn't for children a stop.

The room in the rear was the only niche
That I knew she called her own.
So there we went to share ourselves
And thus feel less alone.

I needed, sometimes, to go see her
But not for her candies, though they
Were the cause I gave to the others who
Never strayed from their summer's play

My aloneness within my own childhood
Found reflection in her aged eyes
I suspect that the reason I came to her
Was that she'd answered the question *why.*

I wonder what she thought of our chats
And that chubby little girl who came
For though I called her my Aunt Lou
I never even knew her name

For me she was just the old lady
Who lived in her daughter's abode
Down a few doors from the lodging I knew
Quite near to the jut in the road

We'd talk, though the subjects elude me
And she'd show me her rags and thread
We'd examine her "works in progress"
Piled aloft her widow's bed

Out of bags of plastic and paper
She'd pull snippets of plaid and stripe
That plaited together for strength and design
Would result in her purpose in life

This braid she'd connect with some other
In a circle for the seat of the chair
That solid, she'd say, to the left of you
I chose for a rug for sweet Claire.

Do you see how to fold fabric under
So that only the brown hue shows through?
If rags they be to others, my child,
I'll create their beauty anew.

I know she must sometimes have suffered
Though she never spoke of loss
Enclosed in that room without ransom
She asked solely for scraps of cloth

She'd attend to my simple stories
While she sewed a tiny seam
And never forget the importance of
My need to sketch a dream

She counseled with her calmness
She consoled when I'd run out of luck
She sustained my faith in the future in store
As she finished a row with a tuck

She'd say who provided the clothing
She cut into pieces of cloth
Those people, I knew, though I knew them not
Would marvel at the miracle wrought

But could they predict (I doubt it)
That their cast-off and ruined attire
Would become by the art of this aged sage
The means my dreams to inspire?

Aunt Lou was convinced that no matter
If materials for being were few
It was what you made with what you had
That created a beauty true

It wasn't her words which fashioned
My trust in the sense of this earth
But her insight that with either the pretty or plain
She could somehow make something of worth

And the value, she conveyed in her joining
Another three cords into one,
Comes most from the joy in giving away
The ministry you have become

Now she's gone though I left her before then
When my growing brought farther things near
My visits became far less frequent
As I spoke what the others could hear

Yet prior to our parting she gave me
A remembrance which remains by my bed
As ragged as the years gone by will yield
My rug gives me strength and I'm fed

For in braiding her rugs all for others
She taught me a truth I've used since
If that which I am is for gifting
I'll discover life's best recompense

Her life had no bliss as I saw it
But her countenance belied that fact
A contentment far deeper than ever I've felt
Sprang forth from her loving acts

I remember my Aunt Lou with fondness
And hope that in some future bright
Reunion between us will help me impart
My thanks for her rug in my life

It helps when a token is needed
To uphold me along love's true way
And transmit to each soul I encounter
The blessing she made of each day.

Barbara McKinnon

Mother

"Hi, Jerry!"

"Haalooo."

"Where are you headed?"

"Out to the Maallll."

"Are you going out to
buy a Mother's Day present?"

"Noooooooooo."

"Well, it's next week."

"I knooooooooow."

"You don't have too
many days left!"

"Weeeell, I mow the lawn
For my mooother and
Shovel the snooooooow."

"So you feel you do
Mother's Day all year?"

"Ya! So I don't have ta
Buuuuuuuy 'er anything."

Jerry's mother
cares for a fifty-two-year old
Mentally handicapped man-child.
She is faithful to the
Subject of her love,
Day in and day out,
Without complaint,
And if not accepting,
At least resigned,
Buys his clothes,
Mends his clothes,
Gives him spending money,
Cooks his meals,
Drives him about town,
Makes sure he has a
Bus pass, good teeth,
And appropriate medical care.

She has no one at home
Other than Jerry
To talk with.

"I do Mooooother's Day
All year long,
Yaaaaaaa! So I don't have
Ta buy 'er anything!"

Mothers do
Mothers' work
All year long.
Gratitude impaired,
Mother's Day penetrates
Our opacity, giving
Us a peephole
To our indebtedness.

While a mother may
Love at time with
Well-meaning obtrusiveness,
Most often she loves
So quietly and obscurely
As to go unnoticed,
Until years later when
We being to rouse from
Childhood and press into
Maturity, making sure
There are bus tickets,
And that each plate
Set before children
Has enough basic food,
If not abundant extras.

Backtracking to the past,
The mind lingers on her
Enduring generosity!

"What kind of cereal
Do you want this morning?"

"Don't forget to put
Clean socks on for school.
They're in your bottom drawer."

"We have to look at material
Sometime, to see what to
Make you for Easter."

"Here's your lunch money.
It's for all week so
Be careful with it."

"You'd better start
On your homework.
Bedtime will be here
Before you know it."

"No, I don't have *that*
Shirt ironed yet!
Well, if it is that
Important to you,
I'll hurry and do it."

"Here, take a couple bills
With you, so when your
Cousin Mary Lynn shops,
You can buy something, too.
Wish it were more."

"Drink your milk.
It makes your bones strong."

"I'll have to call and
Find out how much the
Monthly passes are for
The pool this summer.
We need to be getting those."

"Why don't you do your
Reading lesson while
I'm cooking dinner.
That way, we'll have
Time for a story after
I do the dishes."

"A *B+!* You did so well
On your test!
I'm so proud of you!
I knew you could bring
Your grade up with
A little more study!"

"I think you can tough
This one out.
You have handled harder
Things than this before!"

And the love flows on,
Flows on and on and on
From month to month,
From century to century,
Like God's, from God,
Teeming with energy,
Certain in direction,
Sometimes swift as a current,
Other times quiet as
Gentle immersion,
Driving, spilling, cleaning,
Touching both awareness and
Subterranean areas.
"Shhhhhh! Be at peace!
All is well!"
I am!
I love!

Flows on and on and on . . .
With every race and people,
In every state and country,
In every continent,
Circling the globe,
To the reaches of cosmos.
Some words are common to all—
Mother, God.

Cashel Weiler, OSF

You Mad Lover, You

After all these years,
who would have thought
we'd last?
Gray in my hair,
and reformed by the years,
I've learned to love you
in the most unusual ways—
plowing gardens,
balancing budgets,
going to City Council,
and picking up garbage
with public housing residents.

My predilection for
quick and easy love,
a secure bank account,
and a definite name, role, and address
has never impressed you.

Come,
you say,
and once again I regret
how late I came to love you
and come running, drawn by you to the world.

Theresa Johnson

God's Baker

So many of your friends remember you
This way: a quiet woman baking bread.
Sometimes the haunting smell still lingers, true,
And circles through my memory instead
Of tempting me the way it used to do.
But mostly I remember how you fed
My life another way. You sparked anew
Forgotten dreams until each flowerbed
Became a nursery before my eyes.

Your love discounted nothing: sudden rain
Or summer sun; a swarm of pesky flies;
A bright sunrise; a muddy country lane—
You were God's baker, but your life has shown
Again—we do not live by bread alone.

Carmelita McKeever, CSJ

Miss Billie

She's the rock. Perry's Grocery was always the gathering place for all
the farmers in the area. As far back as memory carries me, the store
was always open and had the general country variety of staples, coca-
colas, candy, peanuts, and so on. Miss Billie had three children to raise
and a household to run, but she was always behind the counter at the
grocery. That is, unless someone was ill and needed a ride to the
doctor, or a neighbor needed to go to town, or someone, somewhere
needed her. And she was never there if the doors were open at the
house of worship! But the rest of the time—you could find her there,
dispensing cheer and a dose of common sense along with the groceries
she sold.

Her children were the most well-rounded kids the world ever knew.
They were familiar with everyone in the neighborhood. Their faces
were always smudged with grease and dirt—evidence of hard playing
in the area where the farmers changed their oil or worked on farm
machinery. They had the best of all worlds—working parents who
were there all the time. And friends—*lots* of friends. And we *all* loved
her. I mean, we all loved her—men, women, children, young people,
old people, Christians, Baptists, Methodists, black people, white
people!

Miss Billie is almost retirement age now, but to those of us who
loved her she never ages. And she still works in a grocery behind the
counter. But it's Piggly Wiggly now. And although they deal in the
same commodities, it's not Perry's Grocery. No farmers playing
checkers or sitting on coca-cola cases, bandying news about. The
sound of happy, squealing children does not permeate the thick,
insulated walls of the Piggly Wiggly. The clerks there cannot and will
not leave their station to take a neighbor to the doctor or help a
confused child with his homework.

But one thing has not changed. Miss Billie is still there. Still ringing up groceries as she dispenses conversation, common sense, and cheer to her customers and friends. Oh, and she rings up love—lots of love—and when you're in her line, it's a bazillion times better than Green Stamps.

Joyce Shepler

Every Time I See an Elephant

Standing in the shower after an exhilarating swim,
The chatter of a lady interrupts, to my chagrin.
I hear about her marriage, her second now to date
And perk my ears to consciousness, hearing problems
    with her weight.

My eyes, with heart, lift slowly, beginning then to see,
Her feet were oh-so-normal, but what about her knees!
The folds and krinks and wrinkles were stippled ever fine . . .
I smiled with deep compassion—and then I looked at mine!

Annamarie Burtness

Woman of the Whole Year

Have you ever known a woman named November?
Neither have I.
Now May and June and April have their namesakes—
Ever ask why?

We rarely picture woman as autumnal;
Female is spring.
Please, someone, name a newborn girl October
And hear her sing

Of harvest cut and growth complete and fruit mature,
Not just of birth.
Oh, let a woman age as seasons do;
Love each time's worth!

Miriam Corcoran, SCN

Web of Life

To weave
a web of life—
or shall it be of hell—
the strands of each are just the same.
Flung how.

To weave
a web of life—
not a crazy quilt make—
takes wrestling with the strands of time.
Flung slow.

To weave
a web of life—
of sacrament with God—
takes splitting, splicing, spilling threads.
Flung down.

To weave
a web of life—
free of tangles and snarls—
takes bending, yielding, opening.
Flung now.

To weave
a web of life—
a textured-beauty wove—
takes burlap and silk, joy and pain.
Flung whole.

To weave
a web of life
takes body, mind, and soul—
spun into shimmering rainbows
flung wide.

Catherine Rettger, OSB

Woman at the Beach

Summer in Chicago:
Sky, water, sounds of traffic,
Different tongues
And there you sit
Knitting on a rock with
Your bicycle nearby,
Your light cotton dress,
White hair in a ponytail
And your youthful back—
All the young people pass by
Laughing
Carousing
Caressing
Wouldn't they be surprised
To know what you observe
As you sit quietly knitting
In the face of changing sky?
And won't they be saddened
To learn what you found out
A decade or three ago?
But they will be happy to
Return to this spot of summer
When their pain too has been
Absorbed by Another and they
Have enough serenity to sit
Knitting on a rock with their
Bicycles nearby.

Ellen Olinger

My Garden

"She has so little time left,"
They whisper as they watch me
Sitting alone in my chair.
A smile comes across my wrinkled face
As I look out at my beautiful garden.

I have lovingly tended this garden
For oh-so-many years;
And, I must confess to you,
It is my favorite spot on all the earth.
But now my twisted bones,
Misshapened by the sands of time,
Are unable to care for just one small plant.
Now is the time for me to visually reap
The product of my many years.
How perfect each flower looks today!
Each one seems more vibrant and lush than ever before.

My eyes drift closed
As I dream of my future.
I think of the site
Where my grave will be.
There, too, the flowers are rich and deep,
And the grass is like a blanket of green velvet.
What a wonderful spot
For my worn-out body forever to dwell!
This package, now wrapped in withered skin,
And tied with the protruding veins of time,
Will then be only a shell.
Like the butterfly,
My soul will finally be expelled
From its useless cocoon,
And float freely about,
Guided by the gentle hand of God.
It will be a soft whisper,
Or bright sunlight,
Or a dewdrop on the morning rose,
Or anything it wants to be.

My dear ones,
Please know I am looking forward to the time
I will leave my earthly life.
And remember that forever
My spirit will survive on to infinity;
And it will be as lovely and bright
As my garden looks to me today.

Karen F. Duh

Harvest

The screened-in porch was chock-full of sun,
    Warm and dozy,
And of the creak-creak of Grandma's old wooden rocker
And the clean snapping of beans newborn from the harvest.
Anticipation of salty ham hock
    Spread on my tongue
As did the faint green stain on my fingers.
Back then, pleasure required work—
    Bone-hard rising early,
    Tilling, sowing,
    Channels hoe-cleared daily
      For liquid life
      To drain from the canal
      Into roots of cabbage,
        Spinach,
        Beans and peas and corn—
    Sun-hot straw hats
      Swished at sweat
        And flies—
    And squirt-squish of
      Milk warm from udders
      Of day-dreaming cows whose eyes,
        Like mine,
      Were half-lidded.
Pa was no slacker—
    Coaxing daily bread from stony ground,
    Praying the harvest plentiful,
    Giving thanks with heart more than words.
And Ma—hands dough-kneading strong,
    Ever humming, hopeful
    As she made a home of wood, glass, and
    God's word bound in black leather
    Omnipresent at her bedside.
Those days, Pa's Ma was there, too—old,
    Worn out from a half a century or more
    Of pushing onward from homestead to homestead,
    From bringing into the world
      A passel of boys
      And seeing five of them
        And her man

Planted in loamy soil—
    Giving back somewhat of that
    Taken out.
Was I ever really so young?
    Has so much time passed
        Since the snapping of crisp beans,
        And hot biscuits with Ma's apricot jam?
Then, I thought it was all hard,
    And longed to be like city folks,
        Parading by the farm in shiny automobiles,
            Flowered parasols coquettishly shielding
                The pretty girls
            While I wiped earth-stains
        From my browned and calloused hands.
Now, I yearn for a hot afternoon on the porch—
    Even for the feel of a hoe in my hand,
    For a dry kiss from Grandma,
    My Pa's bony hand on my shoulder,
    And Ma's light voice chiding,
        "Mind your lessons or you'll end up
        On this farm for the rest of your life."
Oh, that I had learned then
    The real lessons,
    Which now I hold in my urban-dwelling heart—
Too late—there is no time now
    To thank Ma for scrapping calico into Christmas dresses;
    Or Pa for giving me charge and ownership of
        A womb-wet wobbly foal,
    Or Grandma for countless bean suppers and gingerbread
        Tangy from a hot wood fire,
    Or the forty acres (now a shopping center)
        For fat worms baited to bring home Saturday's trout—
They're all in the past,
    But never gone—
        Still flowing in my veins is
            Life bestowed by God
            And Ma and Pa,
            And love,
                Which was harvested as abundantly
                As were the earthborn fruits of the soil.

Mary Weaver

Emma

Too old to go barefoot,
she delights
in ancient soil
beneath her feet.
Dewdrop
under instep.

Years later
she will remember
an intermission
among the flowers.
Taste of freedom
sweet as honey,
last moments of pleasure.

Marita Brake

A Prayer-Poem in Honor of Womanfriends

Let there be in my life those women
who,
knowing and unknowing,
flank my soul with
    courage,
    comfort,
    a sense of place, home, You.

Let them come
    tiptoeing their gifts . . .
filling my heart's halls
    with the food and drink
of laughter and tears, visions and memories.

Let them come
    stomping out the wrath of
indignities, indecencies,
injustices, indescribable agonies
    of many sisters gone before,
    many still to come.

Let them live and move
and take up residence in me (I shall risk it)
where, at last,

I/we cannot escape Love
    nor a goddess named Sister.

Jan B. Anderson

Benedicte

May the God of Eve teach your broken bones to dance.

May the God of Hagar bring you comfort
in the desert times of your life.

May the God of Miriam bring companions to you
on your way.

May the God of Deborah grant you courage
for your battles.

May the Christ who knew Mary and Martha show you
the way of balance.

May the Christ who healed the bent-over woman
heal your pain.

May the Christ of Mary Magdala send you out
to proclaim your story.

In the name of Christ who is the memory, hope and
authority of the future.

Amen.

Mary Zimmer

Index of Topics

Index of Authors